THE SECOND

FORD TREASURY OF

Favorite Recipes

FROM

Famous Eating Places

**THE RECIPES IN THIS BOOK
WERE TESTED IN THE KITCHENS
OF THE WOMEN'S CITY CLUB OF DETROIT**

*Compiled by Nancy Kennedy
Art Director, Arthur Lougee*

SIMON AND SCHUSTER • NEW YORK

DEDICATED TO

THE FORD AND LINCOLN-MERCURY DEALERS

OF THE UNITED STATES

WHOSE INTEREST AND SUGGESTIONS

HAVE MADE THIS GUIDE POSSIBLE

Foreword

THIS volume is companion to a previous one, published four years ago under the same title and composed of material selected from the departments "Favorite Recipes of Famous Taverns" in the FORD TIMES and "Outstanding Restaurants" in the LINCOLN-MERCURY TIMES.

The first volume turned out to be something of a publishing curiosity. Booksellers were never quite sure how to classify it. Should it be on the counter with the cookbooks? The travel books? Or the art books? In spite of the confusion over 450,000 copies were bought—far more than anyone expected.

These books have had an exceptionally long life, as books go. Many well-thumbed copies still stand on kitchen shelves; others, in home libraries, serve as frequent reminders of pleasant holiday trips.

A considerable number found their way into—of all places—professional art schools and art classes of schools and colleges, for reasons suggested by this second volume. Where else would a student go to find reproduced in full color the work of 112 contemporary regional artists, each seeking to interpret local color in his chosen way?

We know there are some very good recipes in this book. We know that many of these restaurants offer you a memorable experience, both in enjoyable atmosphere and in exceptional food. And we hope that your pleasure will be increased by seeing your epicurean adventures through the eyes of the artist.

Dearborn, Michigan   FORD MOTOR COMPANY

William D. Kennedy, Editor-in-Chief

FORD TIMES and LINCOLN-MERCURY TIMES

Your Memo Page

Recommendations of eating places in this book are based on reliable information available at the time of publication. If any establishment does not meet your expectations, please let us know. Address *Nancy Kennedy, Publications Office, Ford Motor Company, 3000 Schaefer Road, Dearborn, Michigan.*

NORTHEAST

A gourmet might well make a career of investigating the culinary riches of this region. He would enjoy Indian pudding, fish chowders, Rhode Island johnny cakes, and lobster pie —all hearty New England traditionals —as well as the French cuisine of Quebec, Pennsylvania Dutch treats, and a sampling from Manhattan's world-renowned restaurants.

PAINTING BY F. WENDEROTH SAUNDERS

Sky Lodge

"LUXURY IN THE ROUGH" is the slogan at this resort way up in Maine near the Canadian border. Overnight accommodations and vacation facilities. Reservations necessary. Write owner, J. Russell Crosby, in care of the Moose River Post Office, for details.

Breakfast, lunch, dinner. Closed December 1 to May 25.

MAINE FISH CHOWDER

3 pounds haddock
6 slices salt pork
2 onions, diced
4 large potatoes, cubed
1 quart milk, scalded
1 teaspoon salt
⅛ teaspoon pepper
Common crackers

Boil haddock and bone it. Fry salt pork and cook onions in the fat. Cook cubed potatoes in just enough salted water to cover. When potatoes are cooked, add salt pork, fat, onions, fish and scalded milk to potatoes and water. Salt and pepper to taste. Float crackers on chowder before serving.

1

NORTHEAST

U. S. 201, Jackman, Maine

PAINTING BY F. WENDEROTH SAUNDERS

County Fair A HALF century before it was converted into a restaurant, this building was the location of a popular county fair. Overnight accommodations and complete vacation facilities are offered here.

Breakfast, lunch, dinner, 8:00 a.m. to 8:00 p.m. Open May 25 to September 28.

FROZEN FRUIT SALAD

4 ounces marshmallows, cut in pieces
1 cup fruit cocktail
12 apricot halves, cut in pieces
12 maraschino cherries, cut in pieces
3 slices pineapple, cut in pieces
½ cup boiled dressing
½ cup mayonnaise
½ cup whipping cream, whipped
Dash of salt

Combine all ingredients and freeze in the freezing compartment of the refrigerator or in a deep freeze. Cut in squares and serve on lettuce with salad dressing. Serves 12.

U. S. 1, Damariscotta, Maine

NORTHEAST 1

11

The Ledges Inn

THIS inn, occupying an old mansion, stands opposite the courthouse where Daniel Webster once presided. Overnight accommodations; vacation facilities.

Lunch, dinner. Closed on Sunday between Christmas Day and May 1.

NESSELRODE PIE

1 tablespoon plain gelatin
2 cups light cream
¼ cup sugar plus 6 tablespoons
4 eggs, separated
½ teaspoon salt
¼ cup each, rum and cherries
    soaked in rum (optional)
2 teaspoons lemon juice
1 9-inch pie shell, baked
Bitter chocolate

Soak gelatin in ¼ cup cold water 5 minutes. Scald cream in double boiler, add ¼ cup sugar and egg yolks, slightly beaten. Cook until somewhat thickened. Remove from fire. Add gelatin and salt and chill until slightly thickened. Beat egg whites until stiff, add 6 tablespoons of sugar, and fold into chilled custard. Add rum and lemon juice, and cherries. Pour into pie shell, chill until set. Shave 1 or 2 squares bitter chocolate over the top.

1 NORTHEAST

Main Street (U. S. 1), Wiscasset, Maine

Long Trail Lodge A COOL summer retreat and a delightful winter vacation spot, this rustic lodge is located near Green Mountain National Forest Park.

Breakfast, lunch, dinner. Closed March 15 to June 20, October 15 to December 20.

FUDGE UPSIDE-DOWN CAKE

CAKE

1 tablespoon shortening
¾ cup sugar
½ cup milk
1 teaspoon vanilla
1 cup flour
1 teaspoon baking powder
½ teaspoon salt
1½ tablespoons cocoa

Cream sugar and shortening. Add milk and vanilla to it. Sift flour, baking powder, salt, cocoa into mixture. Pour into greased, 8-inch square cake pan.

TOPPING

Combine ¼ cup cocoa, ½ cup each white and brown sugar. Spread ½ cup chopped nuts over batter and cover with cocoa-sugar mixture. Pour 1¼ cups boiling water over topping and batter. Bake 35 minutes in a 350° oven. When cool cut into squares and serve topped with whipped cream. Yields 8 to 10 portions.

U.S. 4 at Pico Peak, near Rutland, Vermont

NORTHEAST 1

PAINTING BY DOUGLAS A. JONES

Green Mountain Restaurant DURING

deer season guests enjoy a hearty venison stew; and the year round, roast Vermont turkey is a favorite. In the Pine Room guests can enjoy the original work of some of Vermont's well-known citizens, such as Norman Rockwell and John Atherton.

Breakfast, lunch, dinner daily. Reservations Sunday.

VENISON STEW

Place 1½ pounds of shoulder or saddle of venison in an earthen jar and cover with vinegar, combined with 3 or 4 sliced onions and 6 bay leaves. Marinate in vinegar mixture for 2 days; then wash meat in cold water. Add to boiling water and stew slowly until meat is tender. When venison is cooked remove from water and bone. Dice 4 carrots, 5 celery stalks and cook in meat broth until tender. Cut meat in medium-size pieces and add to vegetable-broth mixture; thicken broth, salt and pepper to taste. Serves 6 to 8.

U. S. 7, Arlington, Vermont

SIMONS VILLE.

ROWELL'S INN

WELLS INN

M. HEILMAN

PAINTING BY MARJORIE HEILMAN

Rowell's Inn For the past 42 years the Rowell family has operated this country hotel which was built as a stagecoach stop in 1820. There is a fireplace in every room. Overnight accommodations and vacation facilities.

Breakfast, lunch, dinner, 8:00 a.m. to midnight. Open May 30 to November 1.

BAKED INDIAN PUDDING

    4 pints milk
    ½ cup corn meal
    ¾ cup Vermont maple syrup
    ½ cup sugar
    2 tablespoons butter
    ½ teaspoon salt
    1 teaspoon each:
      cinnamon, ginger, nutmeg
    2 eggs

Scald 1 pint milk and mix with corn meal. Stir until mixture thickens. Remove from fire and add maple syrup, sugar, butter and seasonings. Beat eggs well and stir into remaining 3 pints cold milk. Add this to hot milk mixture and pour into buttered baking dish. Bake in 250° oven for 3 to 4 hours. Serve warm, topped with plain cream or whipped cream. Makes 8 portions.

State Highway 11, Simonsville, Vermont

NORTHEAST 1

Town and Country

SUMMER and fall vacationists flock to this lovely Colonial inn, which is located near Rudyard Kipling's home. Reservations preferred for overnight accommodations. Vacation facilities.

Breakfast, lunch, dinner. Reservations lunch, dinner. Closed October 20 to Memorial Day week end.

WAFFLES

2 eggs, separated
2 cups sifted flour
¼ cup corn meal
½ teaspoon salt
4 teaspoons baking powder
1 tablespoon sugar
2 cups milk
6 tablespoons butter, melted

To beaten egg yolks add sifted flour, corn meal, salt, baking powder, and sugar. To this mixture gradually add the milk, mixing batter until smooth. Add melted butter and fold in stiffly beaten egg whites. Cook in hot waffle iron. Serve with butter and Vermont maple syrup.

1

NORTHEAST
16

U. S. 5 and State Highway 9, Brattleboro, Vermont

The Ox-Yoke

LOCATED in a pleasant country town, this restaurant, under the direction of Nancy Douglas, has become justly famous for its excellent meals. Try the pecan pie or chocolate fudge cake.

Lunch, dinner, 11:30 a.m. to 9:30 p.m., except Monday (unless a holiday).

PECAN PUFFS

½ cup butter
2 tablespoons granulated
   sugar
1 teaspoon vanilla
1 cup cake flour (sift before
   measuring)
1 cup pecan meats, ground
   Confectioners' sugar

Cream butter until soft and blend in granulated sugar until creamy. Add vanilla. Stir flour and pecans into mixture. Roll dough into small balls and place on a well-greased cookie sheet. Bake in 300° oven for 45 minutes. Roll puffs in confectioners' sugar while hot and again when cold.

State Highway 12, Westmoreland Depot, New Hampshire   **NORTHEAST** 1

PAINTING BY DICK DODGE

New England Inn　THOMAS MARTIN is the
manager of this country inn housed in a rambling building that
dates back to 1809. Surrounded by the White Mountains, this
inn offers excellent vacation facilities the whole year round
and restful overnight accommodations.

Breakfast, lunch, dinner daily.

NEW ENGLAND FISH BALLS

    2 cups codfish, cooked and
        shredded
    4 medium potatoes
    3 eggs
        Deep fat, for frying

Rinse fish with hot water, then press
water out. Boil potatoes and put them
through a ricer. (Potatoes must be
freshly boiled and still hot when combined with fish.) Then mix fish and
potatoes and break eggs into mixture,
stirring as little as possible. Drop mixture from a spoon and fry in deep fat
at 350° until brown. Serve with New
England baked beans. Makes enough
fish balls to serve 4.

1

NORTHEAST　*U. S. 302 and State Highway 16, Intervale, New Hampshire*

Lord's Hill Inn   MANY recipes here are over 100 years old. Overnight accommodations; vacation facilities.

Breakfast, lunch, dinner, except Tuesday, Wednesday. Reservations necessary.

MARBLE CAKE (1800)

LIGHT MIXTURE

    1½ cups sugar
    ½ cup butter
    2½ cups flour
      1 teaspoon cream of tartar
    ½ teaspoon soda
    ½ cup milk
      4 egg whites, beaten

    Blend sugar and butter. Sift flour with cream of tartar and soda and add to sugar-butter mixture, alternating with the milk. Fold in egg whites.

DARK MIXTURE

      1 cup brown sugar
    ½ cup each, molasses, butter
    1½ cups flour
    ½ teaspoon soda
      1 teaspoon cream of tartar
    ½ cup sour milk
      4 egg yolks, beaten
      Pinch of cloves, cinnamon, and nutmeg

    Blend in same order as for light mixture. Butter two bread loaf pans and alternately spoon in light and dark mixtures. Bake in 350° oven for 1 hour.

Whitneys' SUMMER and winter, this inn, set up in a 150-year-old farmhouse, is popular with tourists. Overnight accommodations; vacation facilities.

Breakfast, lunch, dinner daily. Reservations preferred.

CHRISTMAS PLUM PUDDING

½ pound dry bread crumbs
1 cup scalded milk
1 cup sugar
4 egg yolks, well beaten
½ pound seeded raisins
¼ pound seedless raisins
2 ounces citron, cut fine
¼ pound figs, chopped
½ pound suet, chopped
¼ cup wine, jelly, or grape juice

1 teaspoon each, nutmeg and cinnamon
¼ teaspoon each, clove and mace
1½ teaspoons salt
4 egg whites, beaten stiff

Soak bread crumbs in milk and cool. Add sugar, egg yolks, raisins, figs and citron. Then add suet, wine, spices, salt and egg whites. Pour into two 2-quart greased mold pans and cover tightly. Steam 6 hours. Serve with hard sauce.

1

NORTHEAST
20

Five Mile Circuit Road, Jackson, New Hampshire

Dublin Inn Club

SITUATED at the foot of Mount Monadnock, this inn, built in 1787, combines the charm of the old and new to make it a favorite vacation and dining spot. Overnight accommodations. Reservations necessary.

Breakfast, lunch, dinner. Open May 15 to November 1.

MERRITT GEMS

1 yeast cake dissolved in 1 cup lukewarm water
1 egg
1 teaspoon salt
¼ cup sugar
1 rounded tablespoon shortening
3 cups flour
Finely chopped citron, to taste
Deep fat
Confectioners' sugar

Combine ingredients (except fat and confectioners' sugar); let dough rise to twice its bulk. Pinch off small pieces or cut with scissors; fry in fat 3 minutes or until light brown. Remove, place in paper bag with confectioners' sugar and shake. Serve piping hot. These gems are named for the Inn's famous cook, Leonora Merritt.

State Highway 101, east of Dublin, New Hampshire

NORTHEAST

1

PAINTING BY JOHN PAUL REARDON

Folsom-Salter House LOBSTER pie is a top favorite with patrons of this restaurant, which is located in one of the city's historic homes, built in 1808. Vacation facilities.

Lunch, dinner. Open May 1 to November 1. Closed Sunday from June 15 to September 15. Reservations necessary July and August.

LOBSTER PIE (one serving)

¼ pound lobster meat, freshly cooked
1½ tablespoons butter, melted
½ cup cracker crumbs, rolled
3 tablespoons tomalley (lobster "liver")
1 drop Worcestershire sauce
Melted butter, to moisten
Salt, to taste

Place lobster in an individual casserole and pour melted butter over it. Combine cracker crumbs, tomalley from cooked lobster, Worcestershire sauce, melted butter to moisten, and salt, and place over lobster. Bake in 450° oven until topping is a golden brown.

1

NORTHEAST

130 Court Street, Portsmouth, New Hampshire

PAINTING BY DOUGLAS A. JONES

The Northfield and Chateau   THIS establishment is managed by A. Gordon Moody. Overnight accommodations; vacation facilities.

Breakfast, lunch, dinner daily.

STRAWBERRY ANGEL PIE

CRUST

Beat 4 egg whites until frothy. Add ¼ teaspoon cream of tartar, beat until stiff. Add 1 cup sugar and beat until glossy. Spread evenly over a 9-inch pie plate and bake in a 280° oven for 20 minutes; then increase heat to 300° for 40 minutes more.

FILLING

    4 egg yolks
    ½ cup sugar

    1 teaspoon gelatin
    1 cup heavy cream, whipped
    1 teaspoon lemon juice
    1½ cups crushed strawberries
    ¼ cup cold water

Cook egg yolks, sugar, lemon juice and strawberry juice until thick. Mix gelatin with cold water and add to mixture. When cool add crushed strawberries. Spread thin layer of whipped cream on shell. Cover with filling and top with thin layer of whipped cream.

Latham's on Cape Cod

LEONARD and Dorothy Latham operate this restaurant and vacation spot, housed in a 19th-century sea captain's home. Overnight accommodations; vacation facilities. Reservations necessary.

Lunch, dinner, except Monday. Open May 25 to October 12.

CELERY AU GRATIN WITH ALMONDS

2 tablespoons butter
2 tablespoons flour
1 cup chicken stock
¼ cup light cream
   Salt and pepper, to taste
2 cups celery, parboiled and cut
¼ cup blanched almonds

American cheese, grated
Bread crumbs, buttered

Make a cream sauce of the butter, flour, chicken stock, cream, salt and pepper. Add celery and chopped almonds. Bake in a buttered casserole, topped with cheese and crumbs, until brown.

U. S. 6, Brewster, Massachusetts

The Flagship

THIS ship-like building lies over the historic harbor where the *Mayflower* first anchored in American waters. Lobsters, steaks broiled in open charcoal grill.

Lunch, dinner, noon to 1:00 a.m. Open May 15 to December 1.

CLAM CHOWDER

1 pint sea clams (hard-shelled clams)
¼ pound fat salt pork
2 medium onions
1 quart water, approx.
3 large potatoes
Salt and pepper, to taste
Evaporated milk

Use coarse-blade food chopper on all ingredients. Brown pork, then add onions, stirring until slightly brown. Add water and when it starts to boil add ground potatoes. Cook until tender, add clams, and then boil about 2 minutes before lowering heat to simmer for 20 minutes. Season. Flavor improves if chowder is allowed to cool, then is reheated before serving. When ready to serve put 2 tablespoons of evaporated milk in each soup dish and pour chowder over it. Delicious with Portuguese-type bread.

U. S. 6, Provincetown, Cape Cod , Massachusetts

Peg Leg THE dining room here overlooks the ocean. Overnight accommodations; vacation facilities.

Breakfast, lunch, dinner. Open April 1 to December 25.

GLAZED APPLE PIE

CRUST

    2 cups flour
    1 teaspoon salt
    ⅔ cup vegetable shortening
    ⅓ cup oleo
    5½ tablespoons cold water

Blend flour, salt, and shortenings and enough cold water to hold mixture together. Roll out pastry and line a 9-inch pie plate. Roll out top crust.

FILLING

    6 to 7 cups sliced tart apples
    1 cup granulated sugar
    1 teaspoon cinnamon
    ⅓ cup orange juice
    ¼ cup confectioners' sugar
    2 teaspoons water

Heap apples into crust shell. Blend granulated sugar, cinnamon and orange juice and pour over apples. Cover with top crust, sealing the edges. Bake in 425° oven for 15 minutes; then lower heat to 325° until apples are tender. When pie is cool, brush mixture of confectioners' sugar and water on top.

1

NORTHEAST

18 Beach Street, Rockport, Massachusetts

Country Fare MIDWAY between Boston and Plymouth, this charming restaurant presents a delightful blending of Colonial and Victorian décor in a pre-Revolutionary home.

Lunch, dinner, noon to 8:30 p.m. from early March through January 1. Closed Monday during Spring and Fall. Reservations holidays, week ends.

CHEESE SOUP

¼ pound butter
1 cup flour
½ teaspoon salt
1½ pints milk
7 ounces coon or Cheddar cheese
¼ cup finely diced celery
¼ cup finely diced onions
¼ cup finely diced peppers
¼ cup finely chopped carrots

1 pint chicken stock
Paprika to color

Melt butter and blend in flour, salt and milk. Cook until thickened. Melt cheese in double boiler, parboil vegetables in chicken stock and then combine all ingredients. Bring to a boil, stirring constantly. Serve piping hot. Makes 8 generous helpings.

Junction State Highways 3 and 128, Hingham, Massachusetts **NORTHEAST**

1

The Belmont

CHEF George Johnson is responsible for the excellent food served both in the main dining room and the Ocean Grille on the beach pavilion. Overnight accommodations; vacation facilities. Reservations advisable.

Breakfast, lunch, dinner. Open late June to Labor Day.

ROAST HAM WITH CUMBERLAND SAUCE

Boil a whole ham until tender. Remove from kettle and crisscross fat into diamond shapes with knife. Sprinkle with sugar and ground cloves and bake in 400° oven until glazed brown.

CUMBERLAND SAUCE

Mince ½ dozen shallots and put in stewing pan with grated rind of 2 lemons and 2 oranges. Add 1 cup water; cook for 15 minutes. Add juice from the oranges and lemons and 2 quarts of stock, 2 teaspoons mustard, 1 cup port wine, ½ teaspoon ground ginger, 1 cup red currant jelly, 2 tablespoons vinegar, salt, pepper and cayenne to taste. Thicken with flour and strain. Serve on ham slices.

1

NORTHEAST

West Harwich-by-the-Sea, Cape Cod, Massachusetts

Old Grist Mill   THIS pre-Revolutionary grist mill has been converted into a charming and delightful dining spot. The specialty of the house is Johnny Cakes.

Lunch, dinner, except Monday. Reservations advisable.

RHODE ISLAND JOHNNY CAKES

1 cup white corn meal
¼ teaspoon salt
½ teaspoon sugar
1¼ cups boiling water
¼ cup milk

Warm all utensils. Mix corn meal with salt and sugar. Pour boiling water over dry ingredients and stir well. When thoroughly mixed add milk. Drop by tablespoonfuls on hot, heavy iron skillet. Turn and cook other side as you do pancakes. Serve cakes hot with butter and maple syrup. Serves 4.

408 Fall River Avenue, Seekonk, Massachusetts

NORTHEAST 1

The Lord Jeffery

IN THE lobby and lounge of this Treadway inn visitors may view the Plimpton Collection of French and Indian War Documents and the original letters of Lord Jeffrey. Overnight accommodations.

Breakfast, lunch, dinner daily.

HARD SAUCE

    ¼ pound butter
    1 pound confectioners' sugar
    2 eggs
      Vanilla or liquor

Cream butter and sugar. Then blend in eggs. Add enough vanilla or liquor to bring to desired consistency and flavor.

FOAMY SAUCE

    ¼ pound butter
    ½ pound confectioners' sugar
    1 egg, well beaten
    ¼ cup hot water
    1 teaspoon flavoring

Cream butter and sugar; then slowly add egg and hot water. Flavor. Heat over hot water until thick. Serve hot.

NORTHEAST

30 Boltwood Avenue, Amherst, Massachusetts

Alwin and Olga

SINCE 1936 this restaurant, owned by Alwin and Olga Gebhardt, has been famous for its home-cooked food, served in a friendly atmosphere.

Lunch, dinner daily.

OLGA'S FAMOUS CHOCOLATE CAKE

2 cups cake flour, sifted
1 teaspoon soda
½ teaspoon salt
⅓ cup butter
1¼ cups sugar
1 egg
3 squares unsweetened chocolate, melted
1 teaspoon vanilla
½ cup thick sour cream
¾ cup sweet milk

Sift flour, soda and salt 3 times. Cream butter and sugar thoroughly. Beat egg into mixture; then blend in chocolate and vanilla. Add about a quarter of the flour and beat well, then add sour cream and beat. Add remaining flour alternating with milk. Beat after each addition. Bake in two 9-inch layer pans in 350° oven for about 30 minutes. Frost with chocolate butter cream icing.

16 Federal Street (Upstairs), Greenfield, Massachusetts

NORTHEAST 1

31

The Springs

THIS restaurant, managed by the Grosso family, is a popular dining spot. Located in the shadows of Mount Greylock, highest peak in Massachusetts, it offers excellent overnight accommodations and vacation facilities.

Breakfast, lunch, dinner, except Monday.

SCAMPI

1 pound fresh or frozen jumbo shrimp
Salt, to taste
¾ cup olive oil
¼ pound butter
3 cloves garlic, chopped fine
2 tablespoons parsley, chopped
1 teaspoon basil
½ cup sherry wine

Clean shrimp and split to within ½ inch of the tail. Place on a broiling pan. Salt and brush with a little olive oil. Broil for 2 minutes. Prepare sauce by heating butter until golden brown. Then add remaining ingredients and simmer for 5 minutes. Pour over broiled shrimp and continue to broil. Baste with sauce until shrimp are brown. Serves 4.

1

NORTHEAST

32

U. S. 7, New Ashford, Massachusetts

Toll House   THIS charming 250-year-old inn, once actually a toll house, is today famous for its fine meals and its Toll House cookies. Overnight accommodations.

Lunch, dinner, noon to 8:00 p.m. Closed Monday and during January.

TOLL HOUSE COOKIES

½ cup butter
6 tablespoons brown sugar
6 tablespoons granulated sugar
1 egg, beaten
½ teaspoon soda
½ teaspoon hot water
1⅛ cups flour, sifted
½ teaspoon salt
½ cup nuts, chopped

6 ounces semi-sweet chocolate morsels
1 teaspoon vanilla

Cream butter with sugar. Beat egg into mixture. Dissolve soda in hot water before adding to batter. Sift flour and salt together into mixture. Add nuts and chocolate morsels and vanilla. Drop by half teaspoonfuls onto a greased cookie sheet. Bake 10 to 12 minutes in a 375° oven. Makes 50 cookies.

State Highway 18, Whitman, Massachusetts

NORTHEAST 1

Great House   LAMB CHOPS preceded by onion soup and a crisp green salad are popular fare here. Hot corn sticks are served with all meals.

Lunch, noon to 2:00 p.m.; dinner, 5:00 p.m. to 8:00 p.m. weekdays; Sundays and holidays, noon to 8:00 p.m. Closed Monday and July 1 to 10.

COFFEE CHIFFON PIE

1 tablespoon unflavored gelatin

¼ cup cold water

4 large eggs, separated

1 cup sugar

1 cup coffee, cold and strong

1 10-inch pie shell, baked

¼ cup nuts

Combine gelatin and water. Let stand 5 minutes. Combine egg yolks with ½ cup sugar, then add coffee and stir well. Cook in double boiler until mixture coats a spoon. Add gelatin. While mixture is still warm fold into meringue made with stiffly beaten egg whites and the remaining ½ cup sugar. Fill baked pie shell and top with nuts. Chill in refrigerator before serving.

1

2245 Post Road (U. S. 1), Warwick, Rhode Island

Lindsey Tavern

THE ORIGINAL Tavern, dating back to Revolutionary times, was host to such people as Washington and Lafayette. The present restaurant continues to be famous for its fine food.

Dinner, 5:00 p.m. to 1:00 a.m. weekdays; Sunday and holidays, noon to 1:00 a.m. Closed Monday during July and August.

LINDSEY CLUB CHEESE

- 1 ounce stuffed Spanish olives
- 1 medium green pepper
- 1 ounce parsley, chopped
- 6 ounces imported Roquefort cheese
- ½ pound sweet butter
- 1 pound cream cheese
- 1 teaspoon Spanish paprika
- 2 drops Tabasco sauce
- 1 teaspoon Lea and Perrins sauce

Run olives, green pepper, and parsley through a fine meat grinder or blender. Press moisture from this mixture. Run Roquefort through grinder. Melt butter, then place all ingredients in a bowl and blend. Serve in loaf form with crackers. Serves 12.

609 Smithfield Avenue, Lincoln, Rhode Island

NORTHEAST 1

PAINTING BY MAXWELL MAYS

Johnson's Hummocks Grill

ONE of the largest year-round seafood restaurants in New England, this establishment requires eight dining rooms to accommodate its patrons. One of the unusual dishes is a miniature clambake. Henry Johnson is the owner and manager.

Lunch, dinner daily until 1:00 a.m.

BAKED OYSTERS ON HALF SHELL

32 fresh oysters on the half shell
¼ pound each, butter, lard
1 or 2 cloves garlic, finely chopped
2 tablespoons parsley, chopped
1 tablespoon Worcestershire sauce
½ teaspoon each, salt and paprika
1 ounce anisette
1 ounce gin

¼ pound cracker meal
Dash of Tabasco (optional)

Cream butter and lard; add remaining ingredients (except oysters) and mix well. Drop teaspoon of dressing on each oyster. Bake at 400° until dressing turns golden brown (8 or 10 minutes). Garnish with lemon wedge. Serves 4.

1

NORTHEAST

245 Allens Avenue, Providence, Rhode Island

36

PAINTING BY SASCHA MAURER

White Hart Inn

OPERATING since 1867, this New England inn is surrounded by a park which faces the town green. Originally a Dame school for girls, it was once owned by Edsel Ford, who refurnished and redecorated it. Overnight accommodations and vacation facilities.

Breakfast, lunch, dinner daily.

CURRIED CHICKEN

4 cups cold chicken, diced
1 quart strong chicken broth
¼ pound butter
1 teaspoon salt
½ teaspoon pepper
1 teaspoon curry powder
2 tablespoons flour

Boil chicken broth with butter, salt, pepper, and curry powder (mixed with cold water until smooth) for a few minutes. Add diced chicken to hot broth. Make a smooth paste with flour and cold water; slowly blend into broth. Cook a few minutes longer and serve hot with a timbale of rice. Makes 8 portions.

Fork of U. S. 44, State Highway 41, Salisbury, Connecticut

The Spinning Wheel THIS restaurant near the Berkshires is reminiscent of Revolutionary days and upholds the tradition of fine American cooking.

Lunch, dinner, noon to 8:00 p.m., except Monday. Open May 1 to December 1. Reservations holidays, week ends.

CHICKEN DELICIOUS

1½ cups cooked chicken, cubed
1 cup mushrooms, sautéed
2 cups chicken stock
4 tablespoons butter
4 tablespoons flour
½ teaspoon salt
   Mace and cayenne pepper, to taste
   Bread crumbs
1 egg, beaten
   Strips of bacon

Scald chicken stock. Melt butter, then add flour and stir to a roux. Pour scalding chicken stock on roux gradually, beating smooth. Add seasonings. Combine this mixture with chicken and mushrooms. Chill. Form into rolls 3½ by 2 inches and roll in coarse bread crumbs. Dip in egg, and again in bread crumbs, then wrap with a strip of bacon. Oven-brown and serve.

1

NORTHEAST

38

Merritt Parkway (Exit 45), Redding Ridge, Connecticut

Lighthouse Inn and Keepers' Lodge

HERE on Long Island Sound travelers are offered excellent meals, overnight accommodations, and vacation facilities.

Breakfast, lunch, dinner daily.

OYSTER CASINO

6 oysters
  Rock salt
  Crumb mixture: chop and mix 1 onion, ½ each green and pimento pepper, ¼ clove garlic, ½ stalk celery, sprig of parsley, ¾ cup bread crumbs
2 strips half-cooked bacon
  Sauce: mix 2 tablespoons each, melted butter and lemon juice, dash Worcestershire sauce

Open oysters and place the lower shell and oyster in baking dish filled with rock salt. Sprinkle half of crumb mixture onto oysters. Cut bacon into 6 equal pieces and place a piece on each oyster. Cover bacon with rest of crumb mixture and top with melted butter. Bake in slow oven for 15 minutes. Before serving add sauce and a dash of Tabasco to each oyster.

Off U. S. 1 to Ocean Beach, New London, Connecticut

PAINTING BY ALOIS FABRY, JR.

Silvermine Tavern   THE outdoor dining terrace here overlooks the Silvermine River and a waterfall.

Breakfast, lunch, afternoon tea, dinner daily. Overnight accommodations.

HONEY BUNS

Combine 4½ tablespoons white sugar, 2 egg yolks, pinch of salt, 4½ tablespoons melted shortening, and ½ cup milk. Crumble 1 yeast cake in ¼ cup warm water and add ½ teaspoon white sugar. Dissolve yeast and sugar and let rise a little; then combine with first mixture. Gradually add flour—3½ to 4 cups—until dough is stiff. Knead dough for 10 minutes. Place in greased bowl, cover and set in warm spot until dough doubles in bulk. Roll dough out into oblong shape and brush with melted butter. Sprinkle thickly with brown sugar and cinnamon. Roll up like a jelly roll and cut in 1-inch slices. Place in buttered muffin pans that have brown sugar and butter in the bottom of each cup. Let rise for about ¾ hour. Bake in moderate oven for 20 to 30 minutes until brown on bottom. Remove from pans as soon as taken from oven. Makes about 2½ dozen buns.

Yankee Pedlar THIS dining room in the Conley Inn has been serving the public since 1891. Especially famous are the Sunday Buffet and the charcoal-broiled foods. Overnight accommodations; vacation facilities.

Breakfast, lunch, dinner daily until 1:00 a.m.

BEEF STEW PRINTANIER

2 pounds shoulder beef
  Butter, for browning
1 soupspoon flour
6 ounces white wine
4 tomatoes, cut and diced
10 pieces turnip, cut into olive
      shapes
4 carrots, cut into olive shapes
10 small new onions
5 small new potatoes
2 tablespoons peas

Cut beef into pieces weighing about 2 ounces. Sauté in butter until golden brown. Add flour, wine and tomatoes. Add remaining vegetables in order listed. Add enough water to cover and season to taste. Cook over low flame for 2½ to 3 hours. Serves 6 in individual casseroles.

93 Main Street, Torrington, Connecticut

PAINTING BY DOM LUPO

Ridgefield Inn

THIS inn belies the New England tradition of austerity. Its East-West Curried Turkey, for example, is both exotic and tropical. A French cuisine is featured here. Overnight accommodations.

Lunch, dinner daily. Reservations preferred.

EAST-WEST CURRIED TURKEY

Melt ¼ pound butter in a flat saucepan and add 1 pound breast of turkey, cooked and cubed, and 2 pineapples, cut in chunks. Sprinkle mixture with 1 teaspoon curry powder, 1 tablespoon flour, and 3 to 4 cups light cream. Boil 5 minutes. Add salt and lemon juice to taste. Peel 2 ripe avocados, halve, and dip in lemon juice to keep from discoloring. Fill avocado halves with turkey and fruit mixture and sprinkle with grated cheese or Hollandaise sauce mixed with cheese. Bake for about 30 minutes at 350° to 375°. Garnish with sliced mango, peach, or apricot. Arrange with rice. Serves 4.

1

NORTHEAST

State Highway 35, West Lane, Ridgefield, Connecticut

PAINTING BY GEORGE SHELLHASE

Lyons' Pier Restaurant

ACCESSIBLE by car or boat, this popular spot, located on a pier over Norwalk Harbor, was one of the first oyster houses on Long Island Sound.

Lunch, dinner. Open May 1 to October 1.

OYSTER STEW

1 quart oysters
1 quart hot milk
¼ pound butter
⅓ teaspoon salt
⅛ teaspoon celery salt
⅛ teaspoon pepper
⅛ teaspoon mace
1 tablespoon parsley, chopped
1 tablespoon onion juice
    (optional)

Place oysters in strainer and wash with 1 pint water. Keep liquid. Remove all shell pieces, heat liquid and strain through cheesecloth. Cook oysters in this strained liquid until they are plump and the edges curl. Scald milk and add butter and seasonings. Keep oysters and milk hot in separate containers. When serving, place about 7 oysters in each bowl and cover with the seasoned milk.

Merritt Parkway (Exit 38) to South Norwalk, Connecticut

NORTHEAST 1

Sea Village Restaurant THIS establishment
is in a deep-sea fishing port on Long Island Sound. Overnight
accommodations; vacation facilities. Reservations advisable.
Breakfast, lunch, dinner daily.

SEAFOOD EN SOPÉE

- ½ pound filet of sole
- ½ pound lobster meat
- ½ pound shrimp
- ½ pound scallops
- 3 tablespoons butter
- 1 pint milk
- ½ cup flour
-   Light cream
- ½ teaspoon salt
- 3 tablespoons white wine
-   Toast points

Cut sole and lobster into 1-inch
squares. Cut shrimp in half. If sea scallops are used cut into quarters; bay
scallops use whole. Place seafood in
skillet with 2 tablespoons melted butter. Sauté slowly for 10 minutes, then
let simmer. Warm milk in double
boiler. Thicken with flour and light
cream. Add 1 tablespoon butter, the
salt and white wine. Take sauce off fire
when creamy. Put seafood on toast
points and top with cream sauce. Serves
4 to 6.

1

NORTHEAST   *South of U. S. 1, Hancox Street, Stonington, Connecticut*

44

PAINTING BY REVINGTON ARTHUR

Barcelona Inn

OPEN since 1827, this historic eating place on Lake Erie was constructed shortly after the Erie Canal, which brought a flood of settlers through the area.

Dinner, 5:00 p.m. to midnight, weekdays; Sunday, 1:00 p.m. to 9:00 p.m. Closed Tuesday during winter.

FRESH LAKE ERIE FISH

Clean and wash fish thoroughly. Let drain. Roll in prepared Golden Dip bread crumbs. Shake off excess. Fry in deep fryer with fat at 350° until fish is golden brown. Salt fish after taking out of fryer. Serve with tartar sauce and lemon wedges.

STUFFED LOBSTER TAIL

Use about a pound of cooked lobster tail. Remove meat from shell and dice. Add 4 tablespoons bread crumbs, 2 tablespoons melted butter, 2 teaspoons parsley. Salt and pepper to taste. Mix thoroughly. Place back in shell and broil about 10 minutes. Serve piping hot. This makes 1 serving.

Portage Road (State Highway 17), Westfield, New York

NORTHEAST 1

PAINTING BY DOM LUPO

Hudson Shore Club

JUST 39 miles from New York City, this country estate is ideal for people who wish to spend a day or a whole vacation in the country.

Breakfast, lunch, dinner. Open April 30 to November 1. Reservations preferred.

JELLIED CUCUMBER CONSOMMÉ

4 cups chopped cucumber
1 onion, sliced
1 tablespoon chopped parsley
1 teaspoon pickle spice
  Salt and pepper, to taste
2 tablespoons gelatin
1 tablespoon lemon juice
  Sour cream
  Celery salt
  Paprika

Put cucumber in saucepan with 3 pints of water, onion, half of parsley and pickle spice. Bring to a boil and simmer 1 hour. Strain and season. Soak gelatin in ½ cup of cold water 5 minutes, then add to hot consommé. Cool, add lemon juice and pour into shallow pan. Chill in refrigerator until firm. Serve topped with sour cream, paprika, and rest of parsley. Serves 6.

1

NORTHEAST *1 mile west of U. S. 9, Kings Ferry Road, Montrose, New York*

PAINTING BY JOHN WEDDA

Avon Inn   ORIGINALLY built as a show-place home in 1820, this building was enlarged and converted into a hotel about 1880. Today it is owned by Mr. and Mrs. M. H. Hill. Overnight accommodations; reservations advisable.

Breakfast, lunch, dinner daily.

VEAL BIRDS

1¼ pounds veal steak
3 tablespoons butter
1 small onion, chopped
1½ cups bread crumbs
¾ teaspoon salt
⅛ teaspoon pepper
⅛ teaspoon sage
Bacon

Cut veal in strips about 2 inches wide and 5 to 6 inches long. Sauté onion in butter until light brown. Then stir in crumbs and seasonings. Spread this dressing on each strip of veal and roll as tightly as possible. Wrap a strip of bacon around each and secure with a toothpick. Arrange in a pan with a little water and bake in slow oven for about an hour. Garnish with parsley. Serves 4 to 6.

U. S. 20 (east of Buffalo), Avon, New York

Fraunces Tavern ERECTED in 1719, this fascinating restaurant takes its name from Samuel Fraunces, the Tavern's original proprietor, who was steward to George Washington. Washington's farewell to his officers took place here on December 4, 1783. Today a museum is maintained.

Lunch, dinner, except Saturday night and Sunday.

CHICKEN À LA GEORGE WASHINGTON

1 cup steamed rice
1 cup cooked chicken, diced
1 cup braised and buttered
    mushrooms, sliced
1 cup cream sauce
  Grated cheese
  Melted butter

Half fill casserole dish with steamed rice. Thoroughly mix chicken, mushrooms and cream sauce before pouring over rice. Sprinkle top with grated cheese and melted butter. Place under broiler to brown.

1

NORTHEAST
48

54 Pearl Street at Broad, New York 4, New York

PAINTING BY GEORGE SHELLHASE

Grand Central Oyster Bar

LOCATED on the lower level of Grand Central Station, this restaurant is famous for its good food and especially its varied and delicious oyster dishes.

Breakfast, lunch, dinner, 7:00 a.m. to midnight daily.

OYSTER PAN ROAST (**one serving**)

8 freshly opened oysters
1 pat of butter
1 tablespoon chili sauce
1 teaspoon Worcestershire sauce
Few drops of lemon juice
¼ cup of oyster liquor
Celery salt, to taste
Paprika

4 ounces cream
1 piece dry toast

Place oysters, butter, chili sauce, Worcestershire sauce, lemon juice, oyster liquor and seasoning in a deep pan. Cook for about 1 minute, stirring continuously. Add cream and when mixture comes to a boiling point pour over toast, placed in a soup plate. Serve immediately.

Lower Level, Grand Central Terminal, New York, New York   **NORTHEAST** 1

Sweet's Restaurant THIS old seafood establishment overlooks the Fulton Fish Market.

Lunch, dinner, 11:00 a.m. to 8:00 p.m., except Sunday.

NEW ENGLAND FISH CHOWDER

1 pound halibut or haddock
Bones from a whitefish
1 onion, cut fine
½ cup celery, chopped
½ pound butter
¼ teaspoon salt
¼ teaspoon curry powder
Few grains pepper
1½ tablespoons flour
½ pint milk
½ pint cream
2 cups raw potatoes, diced

Wash fish and fish bones and cover with salted water, bring slowly to a boil, simmer covered for 15 minutes. Drain, reserving stock. Sauté onion and celery in ¼ pound butter. Add salt, curry powder and pepper. Then melt ¼ pound butter in a large saucepan, and blend the flour into this, stirring to make a smooth paste. Heat and combine milk and cream and slowly blend this into mixture. Add 1 quart fish stock, fish, celery, onions and potatoes. Bring to a boil and simmer 5 minutes.

1

NORTHEAST

2 Fulton Street, New York 38, New York

PAINTING BY JOHN S. WALSH

Keen's English Chop House THIS tavern
with its paneled walls and ceiling lined with rows of "church-wardens" (pipes) recalls the taverns of Shakespeare's day.
Lunch, dinner, noon to 11:00 p.m., except Sunday.

ENGLISH STEAK AND KIDNEY PIE

2 pounds beef chuck, cubed

1 pound lamb kidneys, quartered
  and cut crosswise

1 piece beef suet, egg size

1 large onion, coarsely cut

1 cup rich beef stock

  Salt and pepper, to taste

  Pinch of cayenne pepper

1 teaspoon Worcestershire sauce

1 flaky pie crust, uncooked

Heat the suet in a stew kettle and brown onion in the fat. Brown beef and kidney, stirring constantly. Add beef stock and seasoning; stir well. Cover and simmer over low flame for 1¾ hours. If the liquid gets too thin, thicken with a little flour and water. When meat is tender, place in a casserole and let cool. Top with crust and bake for 10 minutes in hot oven. Lower heat to moderate and bake until crust is a delicate brown.

72 West 36th Street, New York 18, New York

NORTHEAST 1

51

Mammy's Pantry GOOD American home cooking has earned for this restaurant, managed by Ruth Wagner, a host of satisfied customers.

Lunch, dinner. Closed Decoration Day, Fourth of July, and Christmas Day.

MAMMY'S FRESH SHRIMP AND RICE CREOLE

2 cups fresh shrimp, cooked and
    chopped
2 cups cooked rice
1 onion, minced
1 green pepper, minced
1 clove garlic, mashed
2 tablespoons oil or butter
2 cups canned tomatoes
1 teaspoon New Orleans Gumbo Filé

Salt and pepper, to taste
Buttered crumbs

Sauté onion, pepper and garlic in oil until onion is slightly brown. Add tomato and seasonings, cook over low flame 1 hour. Add shrimps and cooked rice. Turn into a buttered baking dish, cover with crumbs and bake 30 minutes in 375° oven. Serves 4.

1

NORTHEAST
52

122 Montague Street, Brooklyn 2, New York

PAINTING BY HARVEY KIDDER

Sloppy Louie's

IN THE early morning fishermen and market workers fill the old-fashioned dining room of this restaurant, across from the Fulton Fish Market.

Breakfast, lunch, dinner, except Saturday and Sunday.

BOUILLABAISSE

1 medium carrot, sliced
2 medium onions, sliced
1 clove garlic
4 tablespoons olive oil
3 pounds fish in season (cod, haddock), precooked if fish has many bones
1 cup tomatoes
1 bay leaf
2 cups fish stock or water
1 dozen oysters, clams or scallops
1 cup shrimp or crab
2 teaspoons salt
½ teaspoon pepper
2 tablespoons lemon juice
¼ cup sherry wine (optional)

Brown carrot, onions and garlic together in hot oil; remove garlic. Add fish, tomatoes, bay leaf and stock. Simmer 15 minutes. Remove bay leaf; add remaining ingredients, except sherry. Continue cooking 5 minutes. Add sherry; serve immediately. Serves 6 to 8.

92 South Street, New York 38, New York

PAINTING BY WALTER HORTENS

The Old Homestead FOR over 73 years this eating place in New York City's meat-packing section has been serving its famous sauerbraten.

Open 10:00 a.m. to 11:00 p.m. daily. Reservations advised during rush hours.

SAUERBRATEN

- 4 pounds bottom round beef
- 2 large onions
- 2 large carrots
- 2 stalks celery
- 1 pint vinegar
- 1 pint water
- 3 tablespoons salt
- Small handful pickling spice
- 1 cup tomato purée
- 12 gingersnaps

Cut vegetables in small pieces. Combine vinegar, water, seasoning and vegetables. Pour over meat and let stand in refrigerator 3 or 4 days. Remove meat and roast in moderate oven until tender, about 2½ hours. Baste occasionally with vinegar mixture. When meat is done, remove from pan, add remainder of vinegar mixture, tomato purée and gingersnaps. Allow mixture to boil. Strain, add flour to thicken.

1

NORTHEAST
54

56 Ninth Avenue, New York, New York

The Lobster Box THIS restaurant occupies a beautiful 1800 Colonial mansion with a large terrace facing Long Island Sound. It is the oldest landmark on City Island, which is a yachting and sailmaking center near Pelham Bay Park, and is famous for its seafood dishes.

Open noon to midnight daily from May 1 to October 30.

CLAM FRITTERS

1 cup drained and chopped clams
1 cup sifted flour
¼ teaspoon salt
½ teaspoon sugar
1 teaspoon baking powder
1 beaten egg
¼ cup milk
1 tablespoon melted butter

Combine the sifted flour, salt, sugar, and baking powder, and set aside. Mix together the egg, milk, melted butter and clams. Stir lightly into the dry ingredients. Drop from spoon into hot deep fat or oil, fry until brown, turning once, drain on absorbent paper.

34 City Island Avenue, Bronx, New York

Washington Square Inn

ON the northeast corner of Washington Square in Greenwich Village, this restaurant is especially noted for its fish and meat dishes.

Lunch, dinner daily.

TURTLE STEAK

2 pounds turtle meat

Flour

Butter

Salt, to taste

Juice of ½ lemon

Trim all skin and sinew from turtle meat and slice meat sideways to make cutlets. Pound meat thin. Dip cutlets into flour and fry in butter. Salt cutlets to taste, sprinkle with lemon juice, and sauté over low fire until brown. Serve with cucumber salad and lemon wedges. Makes a wonderful surprise fish meal. Serves 4.

1

NORTHEAST

56

1 University Place, New York, New York

O'Brien's on Waverly Hill PERCHED high on a hill, this eating place offers diners a view of the surrounding countryside. This restaurant maintains a farm that supplies fresh fruit, including apples for its home-made pies, vegetables, and pork for its famous sausage and smoked bacon.

Lunch, dinner, 11:30 a.m. to 9:30 p.m. daily.

OVEN-BAKED BROILER

The O'Brien family raises its own chickens on the family farm, which also supplies vegetables and fruits for their restaurant. Their special chickens are fed the last few weeks on buttermilk and corn, which makes them tasty and tender and promotes a golden brown color during baking. Eight or nine weeks is the age limit. The broilers after cleaning are cut in half and each portion is rubbed well with butter and salt. Chicken is put in broiler pan with 2 tablespoons of water in pan and baked in 400° oven 30 to 35 minutes. Chicken is basted every 10 minutes. It is served immediately. A simple and delicious way to prepare chicken.

On Waverly Hill, State Highway 17, Waverly, New York

Lingnan Restaurant A COMBINATION of excellent Chinese food, interesting interior design, and moderate prices has made this New York City restaurant popular. The owner is Kenneth Chen and the manager is Jimmy Moy.

Lunch, dinner daily.

LINGNAN SPECIAL STEAK

12 ounces prime sirloin steak, cubed
½ ounce oyster juice
1 tablespoon soy sauce
1 ounce Chinese black mushrooms
½ ounce water chestnuts
1 ounce bamboo shoots
1 ounce snow peas
2 ounces Chinese vegetables
3 ounces celery

1 tablespoon flour
Salt and sugar, to taste

Sauté cubed steak with oyster juice and soy sauce. Add flour (to thicken), salt, and sugar. Cook vegetables separately. Put steak on top of vegetables when served. "Makes excellent taste and proud presentation," says the manager, Jimmy Moy.

1

2512 Broadway, New York 25, New York

Conti Inn   FIRST licensed in 1758, this inn still carries on its long tradition of hospitality. Overnight accommodations. Reservations advisable.

Lunch, dinner, noon to midnight, except Sunday.

CHICKEN CACCIATORE

2 3-pound chickens
Salt and pepper, to taste
½ cup olive oil
1 onion, chopped fine
½ cup dry white wine
1 bay leaf
Pinch of rosemary
4 fresh tomatoes, cut in small pieces
Garlic, to taste

Cut each chicken into 6 pieces and season with salt and pepper. Cook chicken in olive oil for about 20 minutes or until brown. Then add onion and cook until transparent. Stir in wine and add remaining ingredients and cook for about 15 minutes. The chef here will make up this dish without garlic on request.

U. S. 611 and State Highway 313, Doylestown, Pennsylvania   **NORTHEAST** 1

PAINTING BY LUCY CALL SALZER

Bryn Mawr College Inn BRYN MAWR

COLLEGE owns this inn. Meals are served indoors in winter and on terraces in summer. Overnight accommodations.

Breakfast, lunch, dinner. Tea, 3:30 p.m. to 5:00 p.m. Closed Monday.

BROILED BACON AND TOMATO GRILL

Cook thick generous slices of tomato on a hot iron griddle, then place on slices of toast. Make a cheese sauce by combining medium white sauce and large quantities of sharp Cheddar cheese and curry powder. Pour over tomato slices and toast, and top with broiled crisp country bacon.

LONDON BROIL AU JUS

Sauté flank steak on both sides on a hot iron griddle. Heat the steak through, but permit it to remain very rare. Slice thin and place on warm serving plate. Cover with juice.

The Village Restaurant   IF YOU like Pennsylvania Dutch dishes, plan to stop here. Many of the furnishings made by local Amish.

Breakfast, lunch, dinner until 1:00 a.m. daily.

SCHNITZ UN KNEPP

    3 pounds smoked ham, 8-ounce
        slices
    4 cups dried apples
    2 tablespoons brown sugar
    2 cups flour
    4 teaspoons baking powder
¼ teaspoon pepper
    1 teaspoon salt
    1 egg, well beaten
⅓ cup milk
    3 tablespoons butter, melted

Cover dried apples with water and soak overnight. In the morning cover ham with cold water and boil for 3 hours. Add the apples and water in which they have soaked and continue to boil for another hour. Add brown sugar. Make dumplings by sifting dry ingredients together 3 times. Stir in beaten egg, milk and shortening. Drop the batter by spoonfuls into the hot liquid with the ham and apples. Cover kettle tightly and cook dumplings 15 minutes. Serve piping hot. Serves 6.

28-32 East Chestnut Street, Lancaster, Pennsylvania

NORTHEAST 1

PAINTING BY ERNEST KRAPE

Amity Hall Inn

FOR OVER a century this inn has served travelers who have come in turn by stagecoach, canal, and auto. Specialties are fried chicken and waffles. Overnight accommodations; vacation facilities.

Breakfast, lunch, dinner daily. Closed October 15 to May 15.

WAFFLES

2 egg yolks
3 tablespoons molasses
½ teaspoon salt
3½ cups flour
3½ cups milk
2 tablespoons butter
2 tablespoons chicken fat

2 egg whites, beaten stiff
3 teaspoons baking powder

Beat well egg yolks, molasses and salt. Add sifted flour and milk. Beat well. Mix in melted butter and chicken fat. Fold in beaten egg whites. When ready to bake add baking powder.

Intersection of U. S. 22, 11, 15, Duncannon, Pennsylvania

Cuttalossa Inn   THIS inn boasts an outdoor dining patio where guests may enjoy their meals by a waterfall.

Lunch, dinner, except Sunday. Reservations advisable.

FRENCH ONION SOUP

4 tablespoons fat
2 tablespoons olive oil
1 small clove garlic
3 large onions, finely sliced
1 teaspoon flour
4 cups beef stock
¾ cup white wine
4 tablespoons grated Parmesan
6 to 8 slices French bread cubed
   and spread with garlic butter
   and cheese

Brown onions and crushed garlic in melted fat and olive oil; brown well, then remove onion. Mix flour into fat until it forms a smooth paste, add stock and wine and bring to a boil. Replace onions. Salt and pepper to taste. Fill 6 individual dishes with soup and sprinkle each with Parmesan cheese. Then add cubes of French bread. Brown in oven and serve hot.

River and Cuttalossa Roads, Lumberville, Pennsylvania

Jacktown Hotel

STANDING at its original location between Philadelphia and Pittsburgh for more than 100 years, this charming hostelry was used as a stagecoach stop during pioneer days. It has been noted for its food and hospitality for more than a century. Overnight accommodations.

Breakfast, lunch, dinner, 8:30 a.m. to 1:30 a.m. daily.

OLD-FASHIONED COLESLAW

1 large cabbage
⅓ cup vinegar
½ teaspoon salt
½ teaspoon pepper
1 cup sour cream

Scoop out the center section of the cabbage, leaving only a shell. Shred the center section and soak in ice water for 30 minutes. Drain and dry thoroughly. Add vinegar and seasoning. Toss, and let marinate for an hour. Drain again, squeezing cabbage slightly to remove any excess liquid. Pour sour cream over cabbage and toss lightly. Place slaw in chilled shell of cabbage and serve salad. Makes 12 portions.

The Tavern HEADS of nearly every extant North American game animal adorn the walls of this eating place—a proof of the hunting skills of owners William Everhart and his sons, William, Jr., and Jack.

Dinner, 4:00 p.m. to 1:00 a.m., except Sunday.

CRAB MEAT AU GRATIN

2 tablespoons butter
1½ tablespoons flour
Pinch of salt
½ pint milk
Worcestershire sauce
¼ pound sharp Cheddar cheese, grated
4 cups lump crab meat

Blend melted butter, flour, milk and salt. Add drop of Worcestershire sauce and most of cheese. Heat and stir over low flame until smooth. Put 3 tablespoons of this sauce in the bottom of a casserole. Add crab meat and cover with remainder of mixture. Top with a sprinkling of grated cheese and heat in 300° oven for about 10 minutes. Serve piping hot. Makes 4 servings.

261 Montgomery Avenue, Cynwyd, Pennsylvania

NORTHEAST 1

PAINTING BY ANN O'HARA YEOMANS

Logan Inn

SINCE 1732 this inn on the Delaware Canal has offered its hospitality to travelers. Overnight accommodations and vacation facilities.

Lunch, dinner, except Sunday. Closed January 15 to March 15.

BEEF À LA STROGANOFF

1⅔ pounds top sirloin, cubed
2 medium garlic cloves,
    sliced fine
⅓ onion, sliced fine
    Flour, browned in shortening
1 pint sour cream
1 cup sherry wine
    Salt and pepper
    Boiled rice

Brown garlic and onion together. Dredge beef cubes in flour browned in shortening. Add floured meat to garlic mixture and stir in sour cream. Simmer for 30 minutes. Then add ⅓ cup of sherry and cook until tender, without a lid on the pan. Finally add remaining sherry and season to taste. Serve on boiled rice.

1

NORTHEAST   *Opposite Bucks County Playhouse, New Hope, Pennsylvania*

General Warren Inn   LOCATED near Valley Forge and Brandywine, this inn boasts a colorful history that goes back to pre-Revolutionary times. Overnight accommodations; vacation facilities.

Lunch, dinner, except Sunday.

CREAM TARTS

4 cups milk, scalded
½ cup sugar
4 tablespoons cornstarch
½ teaspoon salt
6 egg yolks, beaten
2 teaspoons vanilla
10 tart shells, baked
Whipped cream

Scald milk in top of double boiler. Mix sugar, cornstarch and salt before adding to milk. Stir until mixture thickens and is smooth. Continue cooking 10 minutes. Blend small amount of milk mixture with egg yolks, then blend in rest of mixture. Cook 2 minutes longer. Cool. Add vanilla. Fill each tart shell with cream filling. Before serving top with whipped cream.

Old Lincoln Highway, Malvern, Pennsylvania

NORTHEAST 1

Belmont Mansion

THIS restaurant is housed in an old Philadelphia home, which was owned by the Commissioner of War during the Revolution and frequently visited by Washington and Lafayette. Today Carl Mai is the owner.

Dinner, 5:00 p.m. to 8:00 p.m. Open May 1 to November 1. Reservations necessary for large groups.

DUCKLING BIGARADE

Bone a 5- to 6-pound duckling. Salt and pepper it and roast for about 25 minutes. To make the sauce, fry the bones lightly, adding some stock. Simmer till stock has consistency of sauce. Remove bones and add 2 tablespoons currant jelly, juice of 2 large oranges and a few fine julienne orange peel slices. Fry boned duckling lightly in butter. Place on platter and cover with thick slices of orange; top with sauce. Serve with chestnut glaze (see below) and wild rice.

CHESTNUT GLAZE

Peel and boil large chestnuts in bouillon to which butter and a little sugar have been added. Allow to simmer until chestnuts are glazed and an even brown.

1

NORTHEAST

Off Belmont Avenue, Philadelphia, Pennsylvania

PAINTING BY SETON SHANLEY

Doric House LUCY FRANCES HUSTON is the owner and manager of this restaurant, which is housed in a lovely old home that was built in 1830.

Lunch, dinner, 11:30 a.m. to 9:00 p.m. daily.

FRENCH HERB SALAD DRESSING

⅛ teaspoon dry mustard
1 teaspoon sweet paprika
1 teaspoon dill
1 teaspoon tarragon
1 teaspoon fennel
1 teaspoon anise
2 tablespoons sugar
2 teaspoons salt
¼ teaspoon pepper
⅔ cup tarragon malt vinegar
1 pint olive oil

2 tablespoons Worcestershire sauce
Dash of Tabasco sauce
Juice of 1 lemon
1 clove garlic or 1 onion, whole

Mix herbs, sugar, salt and pepper well with vinegar. Then add olive oil and beat thoroughly. Add remaining ingredients. Keep cool but not too cold. Shake before serving.

114 Main Street, Flemington, New Jersey

NORTHEAST 1

69

Molly Pitcher Hotel

LITTLE more than an hour's ride from New York City, this hotel is popular as a restful vacation place and eating spot. Overnight accommodations.

Breakfast, lunch, dinner daily.

CHICKEN STEW, HOME STYLE

1 5-pound chicken, quartered
2 large onions
¼ stalk celery
3 carrots
1 teaspoon salt
½ teaspoon pepper
¼ cup flour
¼ cup butter, melted
8 ounces white wine
1 pound mushrooms, sautéed
¾ cup tomatoes

Cover chicken with water in a deep pan. Add onions, celery, carrots, salt and pepper. Simmer for 3 hours or until tender. Remove chicken and strain broth. Return broth to fire and cook down to half original amount. Mix a roux of flour in butter and add broth. Cook until smooth. Stir in wine, mushrooms and tomatoes. Replace chicken. Serve with dumplings.

1

NORTHEAST

70

88 Riverside Avenue, Red Bank, New Jersey

The Afton

CARL WESSLING and his family own this restaurant, which is housed in a 1780 home.

Lunch, dinner, except Monday. Closed during February.

SOUTHERN BISQUE

1⅓ cups tomato soup mixed
    with ½ cup water
¼ cup each, butter and flour
¼ cup each, cream and milk
¾ cup cream-style corn
1 tablespoon sugar

Bring tomato-soup mixture to a boil. Melt butter, stir in flour, and add cream and milk, stirring constantly. When creamed, add this mixture, corn, and sugar to soup. Stir till blended. Serves 6.

BAKED VIRGINIA HAM

Place a smoked ham in a large pot and cover with water. Add 6 medium onions (sliced) and 1 cup sherry wine. Bring to a boil. Simmer 20 to 25 minutes a pound, or until small bone at hock end twists out easily. When done, let ham stand overnight in same water. Then remove skin. Stick whole cloves in fat side, and cover ham with 1 cup brown sugar. Bake in 400° oven until glazed. Serve sliced thin.

South Orange Avenue, Florham Park, New Jersey

Ho-Ho-Kus Inn   HOUSED in one of the oldest buildings in Bergen County, this restaurant has been famous for its food for over half a century.

Dinner, except Tuesday. Reservations on holidays.

CHEESE CAKE

For this recipe you will need: 2 tablespoons butter, 4 crumbled zwieback, 1½ pounds cream cheese, 6 eggs (separated), 1 cup sugar, 1 tablespoon lemon juice, 1 teaspoon vanilla, ½ pint heavy cream.

Combine butter and zwieback and sprinkle over bottom of spring mold pan. Cream cheese and add each egg yolk separately. Cream after each addition. Blend in sugar, lemon juice, vanilla and cream. Fold in beaten egg whites which are dry and stiff. Pour mixture over zwieback and bake in 310° oven for 1 hour. Turn oven down to 250° and leave cake in for additional hour.

CHARCOAL-BROILED BEEFSTEAK

Trim a tenderloin and roll in wet salt until coating is about a ¼-inch thick. Put steak in live charcoal for 10 to 12 minutes. Remove and break off salt. Slice thin and serve with butter.

NORTHEAST   *Franklin Turnpike, Ho-Ho-Kus, New Jersey*

Red Coach Inn   JUST ten miles north of the George Washington Bridge in New York City, this inn specializes in food of English chop-house tradition.

Lunch, dinner, except Monday.

BROILED SHAD AND ROE

1 boned shad (3 pounds before boning and cleaning)
1 shad roe
½ pound small mushrooms, sliced
Salt and pepper
¼ cup butter, melted
1 tablespoon lemon juice
1 to 2 tablespoons white wine

Preheat broiler 10 minutes. Remove head and tail from shad and cut into 4 or 6 serving pieces. Arrange with skin sides down on lightly greased broiler pan or broiler, with roe and mushrooms around fish. Sprinkle all with salt and pepper and brush with half of combined butter and lemon juice. Broil with top of fish two inches below heat for 8 to 10 minutes, basting occasionally. After 4 minutes turn roe and mushrooms and brush with remaining butter mixture. Drizzle on wine, sprinkle with parsley. Serves 4 to 6.

Corner of Piermont and Ruckman, Closter, New Jersey   **NORTHEAST** 1

Saddle Inn

THIS inn is located in the beautiful Saddle River Area. Frank Malocsay, Jr., is the manager here.

Dinner, 5:00 p.m. to midnight. Reservations advisable, especially on week ends.

GOULASH

2 pounds chuck beef
½ onion
1 clove garlic
Butter
1 bay leaf
Pinch paprika
1 small can tomato sauce
Salt and pepper, to taste
Carrot chunks
Whole white onions

Brown meat well in heavy skillet. Simmer onion and garlic in butter until golden brown. Add browned meat to this mixture as well as bay leaf, paprika and tomato sauce. Pour enough boiling water over meat to cover; add salt and pepper to taste. Cover tightly and simmer slowly for 2 hours or until meat is tender. Carrot and onions should be added last half hour of cooking. Gravy may be thickened with flour or cornstarch when cooking is nearly completed. Serves 4 to 6.

1

NORTHEAST
74

State Highway 17, Upper Saddle River, New Jersey

Swiss Chalet THE PFUHL family owns and operates this eating place. The dining room is reminiscent of Switzerland, and meals are served family-style.

Lunch, dinner until midnight daily.

SWISS CHALET NUT CAKE

8 eggs
½ pound sugar
½ pound hazelnuts, ground
2 ounces flour
1 ounce vanilla
2 ounces kirschwasser

Beat eggs and sugar together until they foam. Then slowly stir in nuts, flour, vanilla and kirschwasser. Pour batter into 8-inch round cake pan lined with waxed paper. Bake in 250° oven for 45 minutes. Cool cake.

ICING

¼ pound sugar
¼ pound hazelnuts, chopped or
   ground
5 ounces water
1 ounce kirschwasser

Cook sugar, nuts and water together until syrup spins a thread. Add kirschwasser. While hot, spread on cake.

State Highway 17, Ramsey, New Jersey

NORTHEAST 1

PAINTING BY EDWARD C. GRESSLEY

Croker's THIS charming, homey restaurant has long been famous for its outstanding cuisine.

Lunch, noon to 3:00 p.m.; dinner, 5:00 p.m. to midnight weekdays; Sunday dinner, noon to 5 p.m.

SAUERBRATEN

Place a 5-pound piece of prime bottom round beef in a stone crock. To meat add cut-up celery, carrots, onion, garlic, and a ½ cup mixed spices (bay leaves, red pepper, thyme, basil leaves and whole pepper). Cover with 2 quarts red wine vinegar, and 1 pint water. Leave meat in this marinade a week. Then remove from crock and brown meat and vegetables in hot fat. Blend in 1 cup of flour; mix well with hot fat used to sear meat. Place mixture in a pot; cover with water. To this add 3 bouillon cubes, ½ cup tomato paste, salt, pepper and a jigger of Worcestershire sauce. Simmer slowly until meat is well done—about 2½ hours. Place meat in another pan and strain the gravy. (A 6-ounce glass of red wine will improve gravy.) Serves 8 to 10.

1

NORTHEAST
76

705 North Paramus Road, Paramus, New Jersey

PAINTING BY EDWARD C. CRESSLEY

Gruning's "Top"

LOCATED at the top of a hill, this restaurant offers diners good food and an excellent view of the New York City skyline.

Lunch, dinner, except Monday. Open Friday and Saturday, 10:00 a.m. to midnight; Sunday, 10:00 a.m. to 11:00 p.m.

HAMBURGERS WITH MUSHROOM SAUCE

¼ pound mushrooms
½ teaspoon salt
½ teaspoon soy sauce
½ teaspoon Ac'cent
2 heaping tablespoons shortening
¼ cup flour
2½ pounds ground beef
Hamburger buns, toasted

Slice mushrooms thin. Cook in 1½ pints of water, adding salt, soy sauce, and Ac'cent. Let boil 15 minutes. Make a roux of shortening and flour and add liquid from mushrooms. Cook till thick; then add mushrooms. Form hamburger patties and broil to taste. Serve on open toasted bun with mushroom gravy and garnish of coleslaw and sliced tomatoes. Serves 4 to 6.

616 West South Orange Avenue, South Orange, New Jersey **NORTHEAST** 1

The Country Garden Town House

OWNED and managed by Laura Downing, this eating place opens onto a little walled garden.

Lunch, dinner, except Monday; Sunday, noon to 5:00 p.m. Closed during August.

HOLIDAY SALAD

Color whole slices of pineapple red and green with vegetable coloring. Flavor red with cinnamon and green with peppermint. Serve on crisp lettuce leaves with mayonnaise.

NUT BREAD

1 cup brown sugar
1 egg
1 cup milk
3¼ cups flour
4 teaspoons baking powder
½ teaspoon salt
1 cup chopped walnuts, floured

Mix sugar, egg and milk; add sifted flour, baking powder and salt. Stir in floured nuts and pour into greased loaf pan. Bake in very slow oven—barely warm—for first 15 minutes. Then bake 45 minutes at 325°.

1

NORTHEAST
78

37 West Ridgewood Avenue, Ridgewood, New Jersey

PAINTING BY JOHN S. WALSH

Chateau Laurier THIS hotel was host to King George and Queen Elizabeth when they visited Canada's capital city of Ottawa in 1939. Overnight accommodations; vacation facilities. Reservations necessary.

Breakfast, lunch, dinner, 7:00 a.m. to midnight.

SEAFOOD COCKTAIL

1 lobster, boiled

½ pound each: blanched scallops, shrimp, crab meat, and salmon

4 stalks celery

3 tablespoons vinegar

6 tablespoons salad oil

Salt and pepper, to taste

Dice all seafood ingredients and mix together lightly with other ingredients. Serve on a lettuce leaf with sauce.

SAUCE

Into 1 pint of mayonnaise blend 3 ounces of capers, 1 medium-size onion, chopped; 3 small gherkins, chopped; stalk of parsley, chopped; a pinch of summer savory, marjoram and thyme, and 5 tablespoons of chili sauce.

Major's Hill Park, Ottawa, Ontario

NORTHEAST 1

79

PAINTING BY JOHN S. WALSH

Chantecler   THIS famous resort hotel offers year-round vacations for the entire family. Overnight accommodations and complete vacation facilities. Reservations advisable.

Breakfast, lunch, tea, dinner daily.

TOURTIÈRE

1½ pounds fresh pork shoulder, medium ground
2 medium onions, chopped
Melted butter
1 bud garlic, chopped
Salt and pepper, to taste
½ bay leaf
½ teaspoon nutmeg
1½ tablespoons cinnamon
4 9-inch pie crusts

Toss onions lightly in melted butter, then add the meat. Cook slowly on top of stove 2½ to 3 hours. The meat should not be brown; the pink shade will turn light gray. Add seasonings and mix well. Line pie plates with pastry and fill with meat filling and cover with top crusts. Bake in a medium oven 45 minutes or until pastry is a golden brown. This makes two 9-inch pies.

1

NORTHEAST
80

Provincial Highway 11, Ste-Adèle-en-haut, Quebec

Kerhulu Restaurant

THE excellent French food, liqueur chocolates, and pastries have made this eating place internationally famous.

Breakfast, lunch, dinner, 8:00 a.m. to 10:00 p.m. daily.

STUFFED CHICKEN LEGS

Remove upper part of bone from a chicken leg, leaving enough at the end so that the leg holds its shape. Stuff with a light pork stuffing and stitch up opening. Season with salt, pepper and spices. Sear in butter until golden brown. Add 1 chopped carrot and 1 chopped onion; cook for 10 minutes. Then add 1 glass of white wine and ½ cup chicken bouillon. Simmer 50 minutes. Remove chicken leg, allow to drip and take out stitching. (Leg should hold its shape.) Skim excess grease from sauce and add some *demi-glace* (juice saved from a roast of beef or veal). Press through sieve and taste for seasoning. Add chopped mushrooms which have been sautéed in butter. Arrange leg on serving platter and pour sauce on top. Allow 1 chicken leg per serving and increase amount of sauce accordingly.

22 Rue de la Fabrique, Quebec City, Quebec

NORTHEAST 1

81

PAINTING BY ROBERT BOSTON

Manoir Saint-Castin THIS year-round mountain-and-lake resort is especially noted as a ski center because of its ski school under the direction of Fritz Loosli.

Breakfast, lunch, dinner daily.

COQ AU VIN

1 4-pound chicken
8 ounces butter
3 ounces lean pork
1 dozen small white onions
6 ounces mushrooms, cut
1 clove of garlic, mashed
10 ounces Burgundy wine
8 ounces chicken broth
Salt and pepper, to taste
¼ teaspoon each: cinnamon,
   clove, nutmeg, sage, mixed

Draw and singe chicken before cutting it into 8 pieces. Cook pork and onions in 4 ounces butter. Add chicken and remaining 4 ounces butter and fry on hot fire. Make a roux of flour with a little butter in another pan; then, blend into chicken pan. Add mashed garlic, wine, chicken broth and mushrooms. Season with salt, pepper and spices. Simmer slowly for about 1 hour. Check seasonings. Serves 4.

SOUTHEAST

Southern accents vary with the region and so does Southern cooking. Succulent Maryland crab; steaming West Virginia rabbit stew; a Deep South meal of crusty brown catfish with hushpuppies; Florida's savory array of crab, lobster, shrimp, and her Key lime pie are only a few of the gustatorial treats of this beautiful and hospitable section of our country.

Water Gate Inn THIS inn on the Potomac is furnished with authentic Pennsylvania Dutch pieces.

Lunch, dinner, 11:30 a.m. to 10:00 p.m. daily.

INTOXICATED LOIN OF PORK

1 loin of pork for roasting

Seasonings: 2 tbsp. salt, 1 tbsp. pepper, 1 tsp. nutmeg, ½ tbsp. sage, ½ tbsp. marjoram

¼ cup bacon fat

3 cloves of garlic, cut

½ cup parsley, chopped

Bouquet garni (1 large bay leaf, 1 sprig thyme, 2 sprigs green celery leaves, 1-inch horseradish root)

Claret wine to cover

2 cups beef stock

Rub pork well on all sides with the seasonings noted. Sear it in hot bacon fat containing cut cloves of garlic and chopped parsley. Put pork in baking pan. Add bouquet garni tied up with heavy white thread. Cover with claret and bake at 375°, allowing 30 to 35 minutes per pound. Turn the meat once in a while as it roasts. When the pork is done the wine will have evaporated. Remove meat; pour in beef stock. Brown some flour and mix with little stock. Pour this roux into remaining stock and, stirring, heat to boiling. Season.

2

SOUTHEAST

84

Potomac River at 2700 F Street, N.W., Washington, D.C.

PAINTING BY HELEN FLEMING

Hall's Restaurant & Garden A BLOCK
from the waterfront, this eating spot retains its "turn of the century" atmosphere with original gaslights and an old-fashioned dining garden.

Lunch, dinner, except Sunday. Reservations advised on week ends.

IMPERIAL CRAB

1 pound crab meat
2 tablespoons green pepper, chopped
1 tablespoon pimento, chopped
1 tablespoon onion, chopped
1 tablespoon celery, chopped
1 egg, beaten
2 tablespoons white sauce or mayonnaise
1 to 2 teaspoons dry mustard
1 teaspoon capers
Crab shells

Combine green pepper, pimento, onion, celery and sauté slightly. Blend together egg, white sauce, mustard, capers and crab meat. Then stir in sautéed vegetables. Place portions of crab meat mixture on crab shells and bake about 15 to 18 minutes in 350° oven. Serves 4.

1000 7th Street, S.W., Washington, D.C.

SOUTHEAST 2

85

PAINTING BY AMY JONES

Old Court House Tea Room

"ON THE green" in the historic town of New Castle, this charming old restaurant, owned and managed by William D. Challenger, stands adjacent to a courthouse constructed about 1675.

Lunch, tea, dinner, except Monday.

LEMON SPONGE PIE

2 tablespoons butter
1 cup sugar
3 eggs, separated
2 tablespoons flour
2 cups milk
Juice of 3 lemons
Grated rind of 1 lemon
1 pie shell, uncooked

Cream butter and blend with sugar, egg yolks, flour, milk, lemon juice, and rind. Beat egg whites separately and fold into mixture. Roll out a single pie crust and line a regular-sized pie tin. Then pour lemon mixture into shell and bake in slow (350°) oven for approximately 45 minutes.

Near Delaware Memorial Bridge, New Castle, Delaware

Dinner Bell Inn

OUTSTANDING seafood dishes, Southern food, and hot breads have made this restaurant popular. Conveniently located in the center of town.

Lunch, dinner, except Saturday.

DEVILED CRAB AND SAUCE

    2 pounds crab meat
    2 pieces celery, finely chopped
    1 tablespoon onion, grated
    1 cup bread crumbs

Combine above ingredients and then make sauce below.

SAUCE

    ¼ pound butter
    2 tablespoons flour
    2 cups milk
    ½ teaspoon salt
      Tabasco sauce, to taste
    1 teaspoon lemon juice
    1 teaspoon Worcestershire sauce
    1 teaspoon dry mustard

Melt butter and slowly blend in flour until mixture is smooth. Cook for 2 minutes. Then add remaining ingredients and cook in a double boiler until sauce is smooth. Add crab-meat mixture and cook a few minutes until warm. Serve on toast or patty shells.

121 South State Street, Dover, Delaware

SOUTHEAST 2

87

House of Welsh

SINCE 1900 Thomas Welsh has owned this establishment. Two extra dining rooms have been added recently to take care of the increasing number of patrons. Excellent food and convenient location.

Lunch, dinner until 2:00 a.m. Closed Christmas Day.

IMPERIAL CRAB

1 pound back fin crab meat
½ ounce Lea and Perrins sauce
1 pinch dry mustard
1 pinch white pepper
1 pinch salt
4 red pimentos
1 raw egg
3 crab shells

Beat together all ingredients except crab meat and shells. Then add crab meat, fill shells and bake in moderate oven for 30 minutes. Serve piping hot. For a luncheon why not try this Imperial Crab with shoestring potatoes and fresh asparagus?

2
SOUTHEAST
88

301 Guilford Avenue, Baltimore, Maryland

Maison Marconi   FIORENZO Bo directs this establishment, known for its fine French and Italian dishes.

Lunch, dinner, except Sunday.

LOBSTER AU GRATIN

3 live lobsters, 2 pounds apiece
4 celery stalks
3 slices lemon
3 peppercorns
   Salt and pepper, to taste
½ pound butter
½ pound cooked mushrooms
4 ounces sherry wine
4 cups milk
½ cup flour
1 tablespoon lemon juice

Put live lobsters into boiling water, flavored with celery, lemon, peppercorns, salt and pepper. Boil for 20 to 25 minutes, then cool lobsters, remove and dice meat. Heat ¼ pound butter in pan and sauté lobster meat and mushrooms. Add wine and simmer for 5 minutes. Make a cream sauce of milk, flour, lemon juice, and ¼ pound butter and add to lobster mixture. Divide into 6 individual dishes and top with mixture of 2 yolks and 4 tablespoons whipped cream. Brown under broiler.

106 West Saratoga Street, Baltimore, Maryland

Olney Inn

A CAKE baked from a recipe handed down by a former President's wife is one of the many unusual treats at this country inn, which is located in a Quaker neighborhood. A pleasant drive from either Baltimore or Washington.

Lunch, dinner, except Monday. Reservations advisable.

DOLLY MADISON CAKE

1 pound each of brown sugar, butter, flour, floured citron and chopped blanched almonds

½ cup molasses

12 eggs, separated

1 teaspoon each of allspice and soda

2 teaspoons each of cinnamon, cream of tartar, and nutmeg

2 pounds each of seeded raisins and currants, floured

Blend butter, sugar, and molasses. Add the well-beaten egg yolks. Sift spices and flour and add alternately with the beaten egg whites. Add floured fruit and nuts. Bake in pans lined with greased paper at 250° for 5 hours.

2 SOUTHEAST

Columbia Pike (State Highway 97), Olney, Maryland

PAINTING BY KATHERINE GRACE

Peter Pan Inn   NOTED for its country dinners, the aim of this inn is to "give you food as it was served years ago in Maryland."

Dinner, noon to 8:00 p.m. weekdays; Sunday, noon to 7:00 p.m. Closed Friday and from December 1 to April 1.

CORN FRITTERS

  1 cup flour, sifted
 1½ teaspoons baking powder
  1 tablespoon granulated sugar
  1 scant teaspoon salt
  1 egg
  ¼ cup milk
  ½ cup whole kernel corn, canned
   Deep fat, for frying
   Confectioners' sugar

Resift flour, baking powder, sugar and salt together. Add egg, milk and corn and stir until well blended. Bring deep fat to 350° and then drop batter into fat by the teaspoonful. Fry until golden brown, turning once to cook evenly. Drain fritters on paper. Place on serving platter and sprinkle with confectioners' sugar. Makes about 16 fritters.

PAINTING BY AMY JONES

Milton Inn

IN THE heart of the Maryland hunt country, this delightful hostelry is housed in a recently restored 1740 home which was once the Milton Academy, where John Wilkes Booth attended school.

Dinner, 6:00 p.m. to 10:00 p.m. weekdays; week ends, 1:00 p.m. to 10:00 p.m. Closed Monday.

FILET OF SOLE MILTON INN

Take enough filet of sole for 4 generous servings (more if desired) and cover with water in a shallow pan. Then add 2 pieces thyme, a sliced lemon, sliced raw carrot, a dash of pepper, ½ tablespoon salt and 2 tablespoons white wine. Boil the sole gently for about 15 minutes and serve with sauce.

SAUCE

Heat to boiling point 1 cup cream, 2 finely chopped hard-boiled eggs, ¼ teaspoon pepper, and 4 teaspoons fish broth. Then add 1 well-beaten egg yolk and ½ teaspoon chopped parsley. Stir. Pour sauce over fish while hot.

2

SOUTHEAST

North of Cockeysville on U.S. 111, Sparks, Maryland

PAINTING BY CHARLES HARPER

Shenandoah Hotel HERE is a favorite stopping place for tourists visiting the Shenandoah National Park and Antietam Battlefield. Another attraction is the Skyline Drive, 40 miles away. Overnight accommodations.

Breakfast, lunch, dinner daily.

BLUEBERRY MUFFINS

14 ounces sugar
12 ounces shortening
8 eggs
½ teaspoon vanilla
2 pounds flour
¼ teaspoon salt
3 teaspoons baking powder
1 quart milk
2 cups blueberries, washed

Blend sugar and shortening well before adding eggs and vanilla. Stir in flour, salt, baking powder and milk, mixing until batter is smooth. Add blueberries and stir lightly. Bake in a lightly greased muffin tin in a 350° oven for about 20 minutes. This recipe makes 4 dozen muffins.

Queen and Martin Streets, Martinsburg, West Virginia

Morgan Hotel   SINCE it was founded in 1926 this modern hotel has been popular with the traveling public. Especially popular with diners is the Coffee Shop. Overnight accommodations; vacation facilities.

Breakfast, lunch, dinner daily.

TENDERLOIN OF BEEF WITH FRESH MUSHROOMS

1 pound tenderloin tips
  Salt and pepper, to taste
1 cup flour
4 tablespoons shortening
3 cups beef stock
1 pound fresh mushrooms
  Butter for frying
  Dash cayenne pepper
  Dash Worcestershire sauce

Season tenderloin tips with salt and pepper and roll in flour. Brown tips in shortening and then reflour. Add beef stock and cook slowly until thickened. Slice mushrooms and sauté in butter, then add tips and seasonings. Cover and bake in 250° Dutch oven for 45 minutes. May be served either in casserole or on toast. A hearty meal for 6.

2

SOUTHEAST

127 High Street, Morgantown, West Virginia

The West Virginian   W. J. COLE manages this
hotel, noted for its excellent food. Overnight accommodations.

Breakfast, lunch, dinner daily.

WEST VIRGINIA RABBIT STEW

2 rabbits, young
1 tablespoon butter
1 tablespoon flour
1 cup dry red wine
1 quart hot water or stock
3 cloves
2 cloves garlic, finely chopped
1 bay leaf
　Pinch of thyme
1 No. 2 can small white onions,
　drained
1 cup mushrooms

Disjoint rabbits and season with salt
and pepper. Melt butter in pan, add
rabbit and brown slowly. When nearly
brown add flour and simmer for two
minutes. Add wine and enough hot
water or stock to cover, stir, and bring
to a boil. Add cloves, garlic, bay leaf
and thyme. Cover and place in 350°
oven. After 45 minutes, add onions
which have been lightly sautéed in butter. Add mushrooms and place stew
back in oven for 15 minutes. Serves 4.

Collingwood-on-the-Potomac

THIS country inn overlooking the Potomac is located in an old mansion on land formerly owned by George Washington. Old maps and engravings add charm to this gracious establishment. Overnight accommodations. Reservations required for week ends and holidays.

Lunch, dinner, except Monday. Closed December 1 to March 15.

SPOON BREAD

2 cups milk
¼ pound butter
4 eggs
½ cup corn meal
2 tablespoons baking powder
2 tablespoons sugar
½ tablespoon salt

Bring milk and butter to boil. Beat yolks and whites separately. Pour boiling milk and butter into dry ingredients and mix well. Blend in yolks and fold in whites. Pour mixture into a well-greased pan. Bake in 450° oven until brown.

2 SOUTHEAST

710 East Boulevard Drive, Alexandria, Virginia

Chowning's Tavern A REPLICA of a colonial alehouse, this tavern serves only light refreshments and beverages. The specialty of the house, Brunswick Stew, is a Virginia recipe dating back to the 18th century.

Open noon to 10:30 p.m. daily.

BRUNSWICK STEW

1 6-pound chicken
2 cups lima beans
4 cups tomatoes
2 large onions, sliced
4 medium potatoes, diced
2 cups okra
4 cups corn
2 teaspoons salt
½ teaspoon pepper
1 tablespoon sugar

Cut chicken in 8 pieces and simmer 2¼ hours in 1 gallon water. Remove chicken. Add beans, tomatoes, onions, potatoes and okra to broth. Simmer until limas are tender, about an hour. Add hot water if necessary and stir to prevent scorching. Add corn and chicken, boned and diced, seasonings, and sugar. Cook till corn is done. Serves 8 to 10.

Williamsburg Restoration, Williamsburg, Virginia

SOUTHEAST 2

97

Williamsburg Inn THIS inn features recipes handed down from early settlers. Overnight accommodations and vacation facilities. Reservations necessary.

Breakfast, lunch, dinner daily.

WILLIAMSBURG ORANGE WINE CAKE

½ cup butter
1 cup sugar
2 eggs, beaten
1 teaspoon vanilla
1 orange rind, grated
1 cup whole seedless raisins
½ cup English walnuts, chopped
2 cups sifted pastry flour
1 teaspoon soda, sifted
½ teaspoon salt, sifted
1 cup sour milk

Cream butter and 1 cup sugar. Add eggs, vanilla, rind, whole raisins and walnuts. Sift flour with soda and salt; add to mixture alternately with sour milk. Bake in greased square cake pan in moderate oven for 30 to 40 minutes.

WINE ICING

Mix ⅓ cup sweet, soft butter with 2 cups confectioners' sugar. Add sherry wine slowly, beating well. When desired consistency, spread on cooled cake.

2

SOUTHEAST

Williamsburg Restoration, Williamsburg, Virginia

Sykes Inn A PART of this building was a stagecoach stop as far back as 1752. Today it is a headquarters for tourists visiting the historic surrounding countryside of Virginia. Excellent overnight accommodations.

Breakfast, 7:30 a.m.; lunch, noon to 2:00 p.m.; dinner, 6:30 p.m to 8:00 p.m. Closed Sunday.

DAMSON PLUM PIE

2 eggs
⅓ cup butter
⅓ cup sugar
⅓ cup milk
⅓ cup Damson plum preserves
1 teaspoon cornstarch
1 pastry shell, uncooked

Separate eggs and beat. Cream butter and sugar together and stir into beaten egg yolks. Add milk, preserves and cornstarch. Fold beaten egg whites into mixture and pour into pie tin lined with pie crust. Bake in 350° oven for 40 minutes.

U. S. 258, Smithfield, Virginia

SOUTHEAST 2

Hotel Roanoke

SET IN the midst of its own ten-acre park, this hotel is only a short walk from the business district of Roanoke. Overnight accommodations.

Breakfast, lunch, dinner daily.

VIRGINIA PEANUT SOUP

¼ pound butter
1 small onion, diced
2 branches celery, diced
3 tablespoons flour
2 quarts chicken broth
1 pint peanut butter
⅓ teaspoon celery salt
1 teaspoon salt
1 tablespoon lemon juice
½ cup unroasted peanuts, ground

Melt butter in pan, then add onion and celery. Sauté for 5 minutes (don't brown). Add flour and mix well; blend in hot chicken broth and cook for 30 minutes. Remove from stove, strain and add peanut butter, celery salt, salt and lemon juice. Sprinkle ground peanuts on soup just before serving. Makes 15 average servings.

2

SOUTHEAST *Jefferson Street and Shenandoah Avenue, Roanoke, Virginia*

High Hampton Inn   THIS restful resort hotel, surrounded by more than 2000 acres of mountain park, offers for the whole family varied recreation accompanied by excellent food. Overnight accommodations and vacation facilities.

Breakfast, lunch, dinner daily. Closed October 19 to May 22.

CREAM-STYLE FRESH CORN

2 quarts fresh corn, grated
8 tablespoons butter
2 to 3 cups whole milk
    Salt, to taste

Grate fresh sweet corn a little older than desired for eating on the cob. Melt butter in large deep skillet, then add corn. Cook over medium or low heat, stirring constantly to keep from sticking. Add milk to prevent too much thickening. When corn tastes as if starch is cooked remove from stove. Season to taste. Serves 6.

On State Highway 107, Cashiers, North Carolina

PAINTING BY JOHN A. KING

Goo Goo Restaurant and Drive Inn

NAMED for the famous duck of the late comedian Joe Penner, this modern dining place serves over 3000 people a day.

Breakfast, lunch, dinner, 5:00 a.m. to 1:00 a.m., except Monday.

GEORGIA PEACH COBBLER

1 pound canned peaches
1 cup sugar
1 tablespoon butter
1 teaspoon cornstarch
Pinch of salt
1 quart water
Pie dough for top strips
Melted butter

Mix all ingredients (except pie dough and melted butter), and put in a deep pan. Roll out pie dough and cut it in strips. Lay strips on top of fruit mixture in pan, and brush with melted butter. Bake cobbler 45 minutes in 300° oven. Makes 6 servings. Delicious with ice cream.

2

SOUTHEAST
102

700 Linwood Boulevard, Columbus, Georgia

PAINTING BY JOHN A. KING

Mammy's Shanty

TOURISTS and natives both like this eating spot, located on Atlanta's famous main street.

Lunch, dinner daily.

BLUEBERRY MUFFINS

    1¾ cups wheat bran
    1¼ cups sugar
    1 cup flour
    2 cups milk
    3 eggs
    1½ cups blueberries
    1 teaspoon baking powder
    1 cup Wesson oil

Combine all ingredients except oil and mix well. Stir in oil last. Bake in small well-greased muffin cups in 425° oven. Makes 3 to 4 dozen.

CHICKEN SHORTCAKE

Heat ½ pint of cream and 1 cup milk in a double boiler. Add to this ¾ cup chicken fat. To ⅛ pound melted butter slowly add and blend ½ cup flour, 1½ teaspoons salt and a dash of pepper. Add cream mixture. Stir in 2 ounces chopped pimento, 4 ounces diced mushrooms and 4 cups cooked, diced chicken. Serve over hot egg bread slices, biscuits or pastry shells. Six servings.

1480 Peachtree Street N.W., Atlanta, Georgia

SOUTHEAST 2

Black Caesar Forge Gourmet Club

THIS restaurant is named for the famous pirate who roamed the waters of this area. The dining rooms, carved from native coral rock, are reminiscent of French wine cellars.

Dinner. Closed Christmas Day and June 15 to October 15. Reservations necessary.

RESIN BAKED POTATOES

The chef here cooks these special potatoes over a fire in a cast-iron cauldron with a tight cast-iron cover. A large chunk of naval stores resin is melted in it (about an hour), and Idaho potatoes dropped in. After about 1 hour, potatoes rise to the surface and are cooked 15 minutes more. Then they are removed with iron tongs and each one placed on a piece of heavy butcher paper, which is twisted around it to form a jacket. Waiters cut through paper and potato to serve it topped with butter and hickory salt. (Show this recipe to the amateur chef in the family at your own risk!)

2

SOUTHEAST
104

Coral Reef and Ludlam Roads, Miami, Florida

PAINTING BY MARION TERRY

Captain Tom's Seafood Restaurant

SINCE 1918 this has been a popular eating place. Owner C. G. Morgan operates a fleet of fishing boats which cruise as far as Nassau for sea delicacies. The catch is sold in his fish market and served in the upstairs dining room.

Lunch, dinner until 10:00 p.m. daily. Reservations necessary at height of season.

LOBSTER THERMIDOR

1½-pound Florida or Maine
    lobster, boiled
6 stuffed olives, chopped
3 ounces mushrooms, chopped
1 ounce sherry wine
1 ounce Parmesan or Cheddar
    cheese, grated
5 tablespoons rich cream sauce

Take all lobster meat from shell and dice it. Add butter to moisten, olives, mushrooms, salt and pepper to taste. Braise 5 minutes or until hot. Add wine. Blend with cream sauce and half of cheese. Fill empty shell with mixture and top with remaining cheese, melted butter and paprika. Bake in 350° oven until brown on top. Makes 1 serving.

Northwest First Street and Miami River, Miami, Florida   SOUTHEAST **2**

Island Hotel

OWNED by Mr. and Mrs. Loyal C. Gibbs, this hotel dates back to Civil War days. Overnight accommodations; vacation facilities.

Breakfast, lunch, dinner daily.

TROPICAL SALAD AND DRESSING

4 cups palm or lettuce hearts
1 cup pineapple, cubed
¼ cup dates, chopped
¼ cup candied or preserved ginger, chopped

DRESSING

4 tablespoons vanilla ice cream
2 tablespoons each, mayonnaise and crunchy peanut butter
Pineapple juice or preserved ginger juice

Mix ice cream, mayonnaise and peanut butter thoroughly. Thin with either pineapple or ginger juice, pour over salad and serve.

FRIED TURTLE STEAK

Take 4 pounds green turtle steak cut ¼-inch thick and hack it to tenderize. Season with salt and pepper and dip in flour. Fry in bacon drippings till brown.

2

SOUTHEAST
106

From U. S. 19 to State Highway 24, Cedar Key, Florida

PAINTING BY MARION TERRY

Hanley's Waterfront Restaurant

HERE is an eating place within sight of both the Gulf of Mexico and the Bay of Florida. It is located halfway between Miami and Key West. Overnight accommodations and vacation facilities. Reservations necessary during winter season.

Lunch, dinner, noon to 11:00 p.m. daily.

HANLEY'S SHRIMP DELIGHT

    1 dozen shrimp
    ⅓ cup crab meat, shredded
    ¾ cup cracker crumbs
    Parmesan cheese, grated
    Concentrated garlic
    Butter
    Lemon or lime slices

Cook shrimp and break into small pieces (3 or 4 pieces per shrimp). Mix in crab meat. Place in individual baking shells or casseroles, cover with cracker crumbs. Sprinkle with cheese and saturate with concentrated garlic. Top with a dab of butter. Place under broiler to brown. Garnish with lemon or lime. Makes 4 servings.

U. S. 1, Marathon, Florida

SOUTHEAST **2**

107

Tradewinds Restaurant

LOCATED in the historic Caroline Lowe House, near the southern end of U.S. 1, this restaurant offers steaks that are charcoal-broiled in the outdoor dining patio in full view of patrons.

Dinner, 6:00 p.m. to 10:00 p.m. daily.

KEY WEST SHRIMP SAUTÉ

Peel and clean 8 raw jumbo shrimps per person. Sauté in garlic butter over medium flame for 5 minutes. Remove shrimp and turn fire high. Add chopped parsley and sherry wine to garlic butter. Sear for 30 seconds. Pour over shrimp and serve. This makes an excellent main course shrimp dish that is really different.

KEY LIME PIE

1½ cans condensed milk
6 eggs, separated
¾ cup fresh Key lime juice
1 graham cracker pie crust

Mix milk with egg yolks. Stir in lime juice. If Key limes aren't available use Persian limes. Pour into crust. Top pie with meringue made with egg whites. Brown in 450° oven for 3 minutes.

2

SOUTHEAST
108

Duval and Caroline Streets, Key West, Florida

Candlelight Inn SEAFOOD specialties, such as
Shrimp Sizzle and charcoal-broiled shrimp with butter-wine
sauce, are offered here.

Lunch, dinner, and supper till midnight.

KEY LIME PIE

4 eggs, separated
1⅓ cups sweetened condensed milk
½ cup lime juice
1 8-inch pastry shell, baked
Dash of salt
8 tablespoons sugar
Vanilla

Beat yolks until thick and lemon-colored. Fold in condensed milk and lime juice. Pour into baked pie shell. Beat egg whites with salt until stiff but not dry. Gradually beat in sugar, sprinkling a little at a time over the surface of the egg whites. Flavor. Spread over pie and brown in 350° oven for about 15 minutes.

3131 Commodore Plaza, Miami, Florida

SOUTHEAST 2
109

Lauderdale Beach Hotel   THE vacationist here is offered everything from shuffleboard to deep-sea fishing. Accommodations for overnight guests as well.

Breakfast, lunch, dinner daily. Open November 15 to May 1.

BAKED FILET OF SOLE BONNE FEMME

2 pounds filet of sole or flounder
1 cup water
2 tablespoons sauterne
1 teaspoon salt
1 bay leaf
2 ounces butter
1 small onion, chopped fine
¼ pound mushrooms, sliced thin
½ teaspoon pepper
1 cup cream sauce
1 tablespoon chopped parsley

Place filet of sole in pan, add water, 1 tablespoon sauterne, half of salt and bay leaf. Cover with wax paper; bake in oven at 350° for 20 minutes. In another pan, place butter, onion, mushrooms and let cook over slow fire until mushrooms are done. Then add remaining sauterne and salt, pepper, cream sauce and the fish bouillon. Let sauce simmer 5 minutes, remove from fire, add parsley. Serve over fish.

2
SOUTHEAST
110

On U. S. A1A, Fort Lauderdale, Florida

The Glades THE Evergreen dining room at this resort hotel overlooks the Gulf of Mexico and the hotel's tropical dining patio. Overnight accommodations; vacation facilities.

Breakfast, lunch, dinner daily.

SPECIAL SALAD CUP

1 cup orange sections
1 cup grapefruit sections
½ cup papaya or Honey Rock
    melon, diced
1 cup pineapple, diced
1 cup bananas, sliced
½ cup walnuts, broken
    Lettuce
1 small package cream cheese
1 tablespoon honey
1 tablespoon lemon juice

1 tablespoon orange juice
½ cup whipping cream
    Maraschino cherries

Fruits should be thoroughly chilled and drained. Combine them (all but the cherries) with nutmeats. Arrange lettuce cups in salad bowls and fill with fruit. Mash cream cheese, add honey, lemon juice and orange juice. Whip cream lightly and add to cheese mixture. Pour over fruit; top with cherries. Serves 6.

17350 Gulf Boulevard, St. Petersburg, Florida

Maison LaFitte   IN THE heart of Palm Beach's shopping district, this restaurant is tucked away in a picturesque courtyard.

Lunch, noon to 3:00 p.m.; dinner, 6:00 p.m. to 10:00 p.m. weekdays; Sunday, dinner only, 6:00 p.m. to 10:00 p.m. Open from Thanksgiving Day to Easter.

STUFFED FRENCH PANCAKES

FILLING

Heat a pound of cooked chicken meat in 1 pint heavy cream until the cream thickens. Season with salt and a dash of white pepper.

PANCAKES

For batter, make a mixture of 4 tablespoons flour, 2 eggs and ½ pint of milk. Heat a 5-inch skillet, grease with a little oil and add a small amount of batter, tipping skillet to spread the batter over the bottom. When first side is golden brown, flip over and brown the other. Put 2 tablespoons of the chicken mixture on each pancake. Roll pancake around filling. Cover with Mornay sauce, top with grated cheese, then bake in hot oven until brown. Serves 6.

15 Via Parigi, Palm Beach, Florida

Robert Clay Hotel

CENTRALLY located and convenient to tourist attractions, this is the only hotel with a pool and cabaña club in the downtown area of Miami. Overnight accommodations; vacation facilities.

Breakfast, lunch, dinner daily.

STUFFED AVOCADO RINGS

1 avocado
1 small package cream cheese
1 teaspoon heavy cream
1 teaspoon onion juice

Cut avocado in half, crosswise. Remove pit. Peel carefully. Blend cream cheese, cream and onion juice. Pack this mixture into cavity of avocado. Chill. When ready to serve, slice off stuffed rings about ⅓ inch in thickness. This makes an effective garnish around a platter of cold meats, or it may be served alone as a salad, on lettuce, with French dressing. Caution: do not experiment by adding any chopped mixture to the cream cheese because it makes it impossible to cut neat rings.

129 S. E. Fourth Street, Miami, Florida

PAINTING BY MARTIN DIBNER

Marco Island Inn

THIS eating place is on the Ten Thousand Islands on Florida's west coast. Overnight accommodations; vacation facilities.

Breakfast, lunch, dinner. Closed May 15 to November 1.

FLORIDA STONE CRABS WITH SAUCE FIESTA

Boil the claws of 6 large Florida stone crabs in very salty water for 10 to 12 minutes. Drain and crack claws under a napkin. Serve claws in the bottom half of shells.

SAUCE FIESTA

  ¼ cup onion, chopped
  ¼ cup green peppers, chopped
  ¼ cup celery, chopped
  2 tablespoons oil or butter
  ¼ teaspoon dry mustard
  1 teaspoon Worcestershire sauce
  1 cup catsup
  ⅓ cup horseradish

Simmer onion, green pepper and celery in oil or butter for 6 to 8 minutes. Add additional ingredients and bring to a gentle boil, stirring constantly. Serve sauce piping hot over chilled stone crabs. This sauce is also good with other seafoods.

Off U. S. 41 to State Highway 92, Marco Island, Florida

The Cotton Patch THIS unique wayside restaurant is part of a thriving business consisting of a farm, dairy, and eating place. A delightful spot for a vacation.

Dinner, 5:30 p.m. to midnight daily.

WATERMELON RIND PICKLE

2 quarts watermelon rind
2 quarts lime water (1 teaspoon dehydrated lime to 1 quart water)
2 quarts water
1 quart vinegar
4 to 6 cups sugar
1 tablespoon whole allspice
1 tablespoon whole cloves
1 stick cinnamon
1 tablespoon ginger root

Trim green skin and pink flesh from rind. Cut in small pieces, ½ inch or smaller. Soak in lime water for 4 hours. Drain and rinse. Boil in 1 quart water for 1 hour. Boil vinegar, sugar, second quart of water and spices together. Add rind. Cook until tender and translucent. Add a jar of maraschino cherries, if desired. Pack pickles in hot jars and seal at once. Makes about 3 pints.

On U.S. 11, three miles north of Eutaw, Alabama

SOUTHEAST **2**

Vestavia Temple and Gardens THE

DINING ROOM here is in a circular, pillared building patterned after the classic lines of the ruined Temple of Vesta in Rome. The gardens are decorated with Roman art objects. The temple and gardens are open daily.

Lunch, dinner, except Monday.

ALMOND PIE

¼ pound butter
1 cup sugar
6 eggs
1½ cups Blue Label Karo syrup
1½ cups chopped almonds
2 teaspoons vanilla
2 pie shells, uncooked

Cream the butter and sugar, add eggs, syrup, almonds and flavoring. Bake in uncooked pie shells for 30 minutes, at 350°. (This recipe makes enough filling for 2 pies.)

Almond pie is a favorite dessert among the patrons of Vestavia Temple and Gardens Restaurant.

2

SOUTHEAST
116

2600 Vestavia Drive, Birmingham, Alabama

PAINTING BY FRANCES M. STEPHENSON

Dale's Cellar

HERE a customer may select his own steak and then watch it being prepared over the large charcoal and hickory pit, which is visible from the dining room through a large plate-glass window.

Lunch, dinner, except Sunday.

BEEF IN SOUR CREAM

1 pound beef tenderloin, 1-inch slices
Butter
4 ounces onions, sliced
2 ounces mushrooms
½ ounce sherry wine
Salt and pepper, to taste
½ teaspoon Ac'cent
1 pint sour cream (approx.)

Sauté beef slices in butter until lightly browned. Add onions and cook until clear. Add mushrooms, wine and seasonings. Cook over low flame for 10 minutes. Remove from pan and place in casserole. Add enough sour cream to cover meat and bake 20 minutes in moderate oven.

1927 Seventh Avenue, Birmingham, Alabama

PAINTING BY THOMAS MARKER

The Stable   LOCATED in a remodeled barn, this eating place gained international fame during World War II by serving Ferry Command passengers from every country in the world. The customers' favorite food here is fried shrimp.

Lunch, dinner, 11:00 a.m. to 11:00 p.m. daily.

"FLORIDA FRIED" SHRIMP

> 1 pound 1-ounce shrimp
> ¼ pound crackers, finely ground
> 1 egg
> 1 cup milk
> Deep fat for frying

Shell shrimp but do not remove tail. Split down the back with a sharp knife, being careful not to cut through. Lay out flat, bread with crackers. Dip in combined egg and milk mixture and bread again, shaking off excess crumbs. (The chef here claims most people leave too many crumbs on shrimp.) Bring the fat to 350°, and then fry shrimp for 3 minutes or a bit longer if preferred crisp. Serve with cocktail sauce. Makes 3 servings.

2

SOUTHEAST   *60 S. Bellevue (U. S. 64 and 70), Memphis, Tennessee*
118

Sedberry Inn THIS inn, over 125 years old, is run by the Sedberry sisters and is noted for its fine food. Overnight accommodations; vacation facilities.

Breakfast, lunch, dinner daily.

CREAMED SWEET POTATOES IN ORANGE CUPS

6 large sweet potatoes, boiled
1 cup sugar
2 whole eggs, well beaten
½ cup raisins
½ cup coconut
1 cup milk
⅓ cup butter, melted
Pinch of salt
⅛ teaspoon ginger
8 oranges
⅓ cup pecans or black walnuts, broken
Maraschino cherries

Peel the cooked potatoes, then beat until all lumps have disappeared. Add all the remaining ingredients, except the oranges, nuts, and cherries. Halve the oranges; remove fruit; stuff shells with potato filling. Cook 20 minutes in medium oven. Top with nuts and cherries. Serve hot. Serves 12 to 16.

Main Street (U. S. 70 S), McMinnville, Tennessee

PAINTING BY FRANCES M. STEPHENSON

Roy Acuff's Dunbar Cave Hotel

SINGER Roy Acuff's hotel at Clarksville is a popular summer resort. The dance floor is in the mouth of the huge cave. Overnight accommodations; vacation facilities.

Breakfast, lunch, dinner. Closed September 1 to May 1.

BARBECUED SPARERIBS

2 sheets lean spareribs
1 teaspoon each: salt, black
    pepper, and sugar
½ teaspoon cayenne
1 tablespoon chili powder
1 cup catsup
½ cup tomato purée
1 cup water
1 large onion, chopped fine

2 cloves garlic
½ green pepper
3 pieces celery
    Juice of 1 lemon

Cut ribs into serving portions and place in baking dish. Blend other ingredients and pour over ribs. Bake in a moderate oven for an hour, turning and basting often.

Off U. S. 79, Dunbar Cave, Clarksville, Tennessee

Alpine Lodge THE DINING ROOM here is noted for its outstanding home-cooked Southern food and for its location near the famous Natural Bridge. Overnight accommodations and complete vacation facilities.

Breakfast, lunch, dinner. Closed November 1 to May 15. Reservations necessary for large parties.

HUSHPUPPIES

1 cup corn meal
1 tablespoon flour
1 teaspoon baking powder
½ teaspoon salt
1 tablespoon grated onion
1 egg, unbeaten
½ cup milk (approx.)
Deep fat

Blend dry ingredients together; then add onion, egg, and milk—just enough milk should be added to make a stiff batter. Form mixture into balls about the size of English walnuts and fry in deep fat. The chef here serves the hot hushpuppies with blue channel catfish.

Off U. S. 64, Waynesboro, Tennessee

SOUTHEAST 2

PAINTING BY FRANCES M. STEPHENSON

Frank's Cafe

RIGHT in the heart of a lake region famous for its fine hunting and fishing, this cafe is noted for its excellent fish, which is caught daily.

Open 11:00 a.m. to 10:00 p.m. daily. Reservations necessary for large parties.

COLESLAW

    2 pounds cabbage
    2 bell peppers
    2 onions
    2 carrots
    1 tablespoon salt
    3 tablespoons sugar
    1 cup vinegar

Finely grate cabbage, peppers, onions, and carrots. Add salt, sugar, and vinegar. Mix several ice cubes in with slaw to chill it. Serves 6.

HUSHPUPPIES

    1 teaspoon soda
    3 cups buttermilk
    3 cups white corn meal
    ½ cup plain flour
      Pinch of salt
      Deep fat

Mix soda with buttermilk. Add this mixture to corn meal and flour to form a stiff batter. Add salt. Cut dough into balls with a tablespoon and fry in 350° fat about 4 or 5 minutes. Serves 6.

2

SOUTHEAST

122

On U. S. 70, 4 miles east of Camden, Tennessee

PAINTING BY JOHN A. KING

The Glass House   At the foot of Lookout Mountain, near Signal Mountain and the Chickamauga Battle Grounds, this restaurant is one of a chain in the South.

Breakfast, lunch, dinner daily.

COCONUT CREAM PIE

2 large eggs
1 pint milk
1 cup sugar
Pinch of salt
2 heaping tablespoons cornstarch
1 tablespoon butter
½ teaspoon vanilla
1 8-inch pie shell, baked
1 cup coconut, shredded

Separate eggs, saving whites for meringue. Beat yolks into ¾ cup of milk, adding sugar and salt. Heat in double boiler. Mix cornstarch and remaining milk and blend with first milk mixture. Add butter. Stir until this mixture thickens and sticks to spoon. Remove from fire and add vanilla. Pour half of cream filling into pie shell and sprinkle with coconut. Add remaining filling and sprinkle with additional coconut. Cover pie with meringue made with egg whites. Sprinkle remaining coconut over top. Put in 350° oven until meringue and coconut are browned.

3300 Broad Street (U. S. 41), Chattanooga, Tennessee   **SOUTHEAST**   **2**

Montgomery Bell Inn   OWNED and operated
by the State of Tennessee, this restaurant is in beautiful Montgomery Bell State Park, about 36 miles west of Nashville. Overnight accommodations.

Breakfast, lunch, dinner daily.

SWEET POTATO DELIGHT

6 large yams
½ pound butter
1½ cups sugar
3 cups orange juice
1½ cups chopped black walnuts
Marshmallows

Peel potatoes and slice crosswise. Cook until tender in as little water as possible. Drain water and whip potatoes until creamy. Add other ingredients (except marshmallows) and mix well. Place in baking dish and top with marshmallows. Brown in oven for about 10 minutes. Serve piping hot. Serves 12.

PAINTING BY CHARLES HARPER

Ashbourne Inn THIS establishment is located in a frame building, built in 1845, on the historic Berry Taylor place. Native stone has been added to the exterior, and the interior has been furnished with antiques. Overnight accommodations and vacation facilities.

Breakfast, lunch, dinner. Closed Monday and during the winter months.

WAFFLES

    1 level teaspoon baking soda
    1 teaspoon baking powder
    1 level teaspoon salt
    2 cups flour
    ½ cup Wesson oil
    3 eggs
    1½ cups buttermilk

Sift dry ingredients together. Add oil and eggs and beat well. Stir in buttermilk. (It may be necessary to use more buttermilk if batter is very thick.) When waffles are baked place on a rack in a warm oven to crisp before serving. At the Inn the waffles are served with butter, maple syrup, and chicken hash.

PAINTING BY CHARLES HARPER

Capps Coach House Mr. and Mrs. Olen

Capps own and manage this eating place which they started with the idea of giving the Blue Grass country a "horsey" restaurant. It is located adjacent to the world famous Tattersall's, where horse auctions have been held for over 75 years.

Lunch, dinner daily.

COACH HOUSE HOT BROWN

For each portion remove crust from a well-toasted slice of white bread, cut bread diagonally, and place halves on oven-proof plate. Cover toast with either chicken or turkey sliced very thin. Cover this with your favorite medium cream sauce, sprinkle with sliced fresh mushrooms and Parmesan cheese and a dash of paprika. Edge the cream sauce with 4 cubes of fresh tomato. Place under broiler until cream sauce starts to bubble. Then remove and cross plate with partly cooked bacon. Return to the broiler until plate is very hot. Garnish with a sprig of parsley. This is a wonderful way to make a party dish of leftover holiday fowl.

2

SOUTHEAST   *855 South Broadway (U. S. 68), Lexington, Kentucky*
126

NORTH CENTRAL

Fertile farm lands, huge dairy herds, vast orchards, and countless fish-filled lakes are a delight to the vacationist's eye and eventually to his palate. Fresh-water fish are served fried, baked, sweet and sour, and pickled. Rich layer cake and tortes are topped with a dollop of whipped cream, apple pie with a serving of butter-yellow vanilla ice cream.

Wabun

THE SHORES of Lake Huron make this establishment a perfect summer or fall vacation spot. Overnight accommodations; vacation facilities.

Breakfast, lunch, dinner daily. Closed December 1 to May 1. Reservations advisable on Saturday.

TUNA NOODLE CASSEROLE

1 small onion, sliced thin
Butter
1 can or 2 cups homemade fried noodles
1 can tuna, 13 ounces
1 can mushroom soup
Pepper
¼ pound potato chips, crushed

Sauté onion in butter until it is a golden brown. Place half the noodles in a greased casserole dish, spread with layer of onion, tuna fish and mushroom soup. Top with remaining noodles and sprinkle top with pepper and potato chips. Bake in 325° oven for about a half hour or until thick and brown. Serves 4.

U. S. 23, Oscoda, Michigan

Al Green's

THIS eating place, in a suburb of Detroit, has been popular for many years. The food and service are excellent. A favorite dish is Chicken Cacciatore.

Lunch, dinner until 2:00 a.m. daily.

CHICKEN CACCIATORE

2 fryers, disjointed
Olive oil
2 large onions, chopped
1 pound mushrooms, sliced
1 No. 2½ can tomatoes
1 clove garlic
1 tablespoon oregano
1 tablespoon salt
Black pepper, to taste
1 cup Rhine wine

1 cup chicken stock
½ cup pitted, sliced green olives
Mastaccioli noodles

Sauté chicken in olive oil till brown. Add onions, mushrooms, tomatoes, garlic, oregano, salt, pepper. Brown slightly. Add wine and simmer for 20 minutes. Add chicken stock, reduce heat and add sliced olives. Serve with noodles. Serves 6.

PAINTING BY KING CALKINS

Hotel Mayflower MANAGED by Ralph Lorenz,

this is one of Michigan's outstanding small hotels. The Mayflower Room, with its life-size reproductions of famous mas-
terpieces depicting Pilgrim history, is a favorite stopping place
for diners who enjoy good food in restful surroundings. Overnight accommodations.

Breakfast, lunch, dinner daily.

SPICED CARROTS

2 quarts carrots
1 quart white vinegar
½ cup mixed pickling spices
1 cup sugar
1 teaspoon Maggi (made by Nestle
Company, White Plains, New
York)

Cook carrots whole or in chunks and
let cool. Bring vinegar, spices, sugar
and Maggi to a boil. Pour over carrots
while vinegar mixture is still hot. Let
stand overnight. At the hotel this is
one of the most popular relishes served.
Try it with lamb or veal.

3

NORTH CENTRAL   *827 West Ann Arbor Trail, Plymouth, Michigan*

130

Hotel Dilworth OWNED and managed by Mr. and Mrs. Don Sheets, this hotel is located in a noted Michigan winter and summer vacation area. Overnight accommodations and complete vacation facilities are offered.

Breakfast, 7:00 a.m. to 9:30 a.m., dinner, 6:00 p.m. to 8:00 p.m. weekdays; Sunday, breakfast, 8:00 a.m. to 10:00 a.m., dinner, 1:00 p.m. to 3:00 p.m.

TOMATO PUDDING

   1 cup brown sugar

   ¾ cup boiling water

   ½ teaspoon salt

   1 10-ounce can of tomato purée

   1 cup bread, diced

   ½ cup melted butter

Add sugar, water and salt to tomato purée. Boil 5 minutes. Place bread squares in a casserole and pour melted butter over them. Add hot tomato mixture and place cover on casserole. Bake in a moderate oven, about 350°, for 30 minutes. This dish appears as an entrée condiment rather than as a dessert on the hotel's menu.

State Highway 75, Boyne City, Michigan

NORTH CENTRAL 3

Bessie Miller's Broadview Club THIS
eating place, located in a 150-year-old farmhouse, is justly
famous for its clambakes and chicken dinners.

Dinner, 5:30 p.m. to 9:30 p.m. weekdays; Sunday, 12:30 p.m. to 8:00 p.m.
Closed Monday and November 1 to May 1. Reservations advisable.

CORN FRITTERS

2 cups cream-style corn

6 cups flour

1 teaspoon salt

2 tablespoons sugar

1 quart milk

4 eggs, separated

2 tablespoons baking powder

Hot lard, for frying

Blend all ingredients together except
egg whites and lard. Beat egg whites
and fold into dough mixture. Heat inch-
deep lard in heavy iron skillet over a
moderate flame. Drop 1 tablespoon dough
mixture into lard for each fritter. Brown
on one side, turn. Then place skillet
with fritters in 450° oven for about 2
minutes before serving. Makes 50.

3 NORTH CENTRAL

6048 Broadview Road, Parma, Ohio

Terrace Plaza Hotel THE TERRACE GARDEN
dining room here opens onto an outdoor terrace in summer and
a skating rink in winter. Overnight accommodations.

Breakfast, lunch, and cocktails weekdays; Sunday, breakfast only.

SCALLOPINI OF VEAL ON RICE ALBUFERA

4 veal steaks, 6 ounces apiece
1 tablespoon onion, chopped
1 cup rice, raw
¼ pound butter
2 cups chicken broth
1 chicken liver
2 mushrooms
  Salt and pepper
  Flour
1 tablespoon shredded almonds

Fry onions and rice in part of butter
until brown. Add broth; cover and bake
in oven 18 to 20 minutes without stirring. Parboil chicken liver. Dice and
fry liver and mushrooms, then combine
with rice in oven. Halve veal steaks;
season and flour lightly before sautéing
in more of butter until well done. Serve
2 steak halves on each portion of Rice
Albufera. Top with almonds sautéed in
remaining butter until brown.

Sixth and Vine Streets, Cincinnati, Ohio

NORTH CENTRAL 3

PAINTING BY EDWIN FULWIDER

Village Inn   NEAR Kenyon College, this inn features one-man art shows of local and regional artists.

Breakfast, lunch, dinner. Also open 8:00 p.m. to 11:00 p.m. during school year. Closed Monday and holidays.

CELERY SEED DRESSING

Mix together ½ cup sugar, 1 teaspoon dry mustard, 1 teaspoon salt, and ¼ grated onion. Then take ⅓ cup vinegar and 1 cup salad oil. Add a little bit of vinegar to mixture and blend thoroughly. Add vinegar and oil alternately and beat well. Add 1 tablespoon celery seed. Cover and store in refrigerator. Excellent on fruit salad.

MOLDED CRANBERRY SALAD

½ cup strawberry gelatin
1 cup boiling water
1 cup cranberry sauce, strained
½ cup apples, chopped
½ cup celery, chopped
¼ cup nuts, chopped

Dissolve gelatin in boiling water. Add cranberry sauce and whip to dissolve. Cool, add apples, celery and nuts. Chill. Serve in squares on lettuce with salad dressing.

On State Highway 229, Gambier, Ohio

3

NORTH CENTRAL
134

Hoffman's Garden

THIS restaurant is conveniently located on the main highway. A smörgåsbord table is featured here every evening from 5:00 p.m. to 10:00 p.m.

Lunch, dinner, 11:00 a.m. to 1:00 a.m., except Sunday.

CHOP SUEY SALAD

2 cups cooked meat, cubed
2 cups cooked red kidney beans
¼ cup diced red pimento
1 cup diced celery
½ cup diced onions
2 cups bean sprouts (marinated in French dressing)
Chop suey sauce, to taste

Salt and pepper, to taste
½ cup mayonnaise

Add ingredients in order given and mix thoroughly in the salad bowl. Makes a tasty luncheon meal by itself or may be served as the dinner salad course. Try it when you have some left-over meat.

Hotel Lafayette

HISTORIC pictures and a priceless collection of muzzle-loading rifles hang on the knotty pine walls of the Gun Room, a favorite dining spot in this hotel. Overnight accommodations; vacation facilities.

Breakfast, lunch, dinner, 7:00 a.m. to midnight weekdays; Sunday, 7:30 a.m. to 9:00 p.m.

COCKTAIL SANDWICHES

3 hard-boiled eggs
18 small stuffed olives
2 thin slices Bermuda onion
1 heaping tablespoon mustard
Salt and pepper, to taste
Thin bread or crackers

Chop and then grind into paste the eggs, olives and onion. Blend in mustard and salt and pepper to taste. Spread on very thin bread slices or crackers. Also makes a good filling for a closed sandwich garnished with lettuce.

3

NORTH CENTRAL
136

101-111 Front Street, Marietta, Ohio

Pete's Wayside Inn

OWNED and managed by Mr. and Mrs. Arthur Mack, this attractive inn is a popular dining place in the Cleveland area.

Breakfast, lunch, dinner, 9:00 a.m. to 1:00 a.m. daily.

CHICKEN PAPRIKASH

4-pound spring chicken
3 medium onions, sliced
2 tablespoons paprika
1 tablespoon shortening
2 cups broth or cold water
3 tablespoons flour
⅛ teaspoon red pepper
1 tablespoon salt
½ cup sour cream

Sauté onions and paprika in shortening slowly for 10 minutes. Add disjointed chicken. Cover pan; simmer slowly until golden brown. Add broth; cook till tender—1 to 1½ hours. Add water if needed. Blend flour, seasonings and sour cream about 5 minutes before chicken is done. Stir into chicken mixture slowly. Serve with dumplings or noodles.

Brookpark and Ridge Roads, Cleveland, Ohio

PAINTING BY PETER PAUL DUBANIEWICZ

Luccioni's

THIS restaurant, noted for its fine Italian food, has been in the same location in downtown Cleveland for over 30 years. Florindo Luccioni is the owner.

Lunch, dinner until 1:00 a.m. Closed Sunday and holidays.

DELICIOUS THIRTY-MINUTE SAUCE

¼ pound butter

4 tablespoons olive oil

½ onion, chopped

1 clove garlic, chopped

1 small piece celery, chopped

1 small carrot, chopped

2 sprigs parsley, chopped

1 No. 2 can tomatoes

Salt and pepper, to taste

3 tablespoons Parmesan cheese, grated

Heat butter and oil together and add to it all chopped ingredients. Fry until golden brown or until onions are soft. Add tomatoes. Cook over medium fire for about 20 minutes more, stirring occasionally. Add seasonings and cheese. This amount will be enough to serve with a pound of spaghetti.

3

NORTH CENTRAL

4213 Euclid Avenue, Cleveland, Ohio

Smörgåsbord

OVER 125 different dishes are attractively displayed on this restaurant's smörgåsbord table, which is 20 feet long.

Lunch, dinner, except Monday. Reservations advisable.

BREAD PUDDING

Rolls or bread slices, 6 cups
when quartered (approx.)
8 eggs, separated
1½ pints cream
½ cup sugar, plus 2 tablespoons
for meringue
Juice of ½ orange
Rind of ½ orange

Quarter the rolls or bread slices until you have enough to fill an 8 x 11-inch baking dish completely. Beat egg yolks; add cream, ½ cup sugar; mix thoroughly. Pour mixture over bread. Combine orange juice and rind; pour over mixture. Bake in preheated 300° oven for 1 hour. Beat egg whites until stiff, then slowly add 2 tablespoons sugar. When bread pudding is done, spread top with egg whites. Bake in preheated 275° oven for about 20 minutes. If desired, sprinkle top with nutmeats. Serves 10 to 12 people.

3983 Darrow Road (State Highway 91), Stow, Ohio

NORTH CENTRAL

PAINTING BY J. P. OLMES

The Golden Lamb ONE OF Ohio's oldest, this hotel was host to such people as Charles Dickens and Henry Clay. Overnight accommodations.

Breakfast, lunch, dinner weekdays; Sunday and holidays, dinner only, noon to 8:00 p.m. Closed Christmas Day. Reservations advisable.

STRAWBERRY TORTE

To make torte, beat ¼ cup butter, ½ cup sifted sugar, 4 egg yolks, ½ teaspoon vanilla, 1 cup cake flour, 2 teaspoons baking powder, and ⅓ cup cream until smooth. Spread mixture in two 9-inch pans. Beat 4 egg whites until stiff. Gradually blend in 1 cup sugar, beating continuously. Add ½ teaspoon vanilla to flavor. Spread this meringue over torte. Bake torte and meringue in very slow oven for 30 minutes. Let cool in pans.

Make a filling of 1 cup crushed, sweetened strawberries blended with ½ pint whipping cream, whipped. Just before serving, place 1 torte on plate, meringue side down, and cover with half of filling. Add top layer of torte, and top with remaining filling. Serves 12.

Mecklenburg's Garden Delicious German dishes are the specialty at this Cincinnati landmark. Meals are served in an outdoor garden in warm weather and in an attractive dining room in the winter.

Lunch, dinner daily.

POTATO PANCAKES

5 uncooked potatoes
1 medium onion
½ teaspoon salt
Dash of pepper
2 eggs
1 tablespoon parsley, chopped
2 tablespoons flour

Grate potatoes and onion. Add salt, pepper, eggs, parsley and flour. Mix well and drop by tablespoonfuls into very hot fat in a heavy frying pan. Fry until golden brown, turning once. Serves 6. Try these pancakes with sauerbraten.

Gruber's

IN THE suburb of Shaker Heights, outside of Cleveland, this restaurant has been famous for many years as one of the top eating places in the area.

Dinner, 5:00 p.m. to 1:00 a.m., except Sunday. Reservations necessary.

BAKED SPINACH SOUFFLÉ

2 pounds fresh, cooked spinach, finely chopped

3 tablespoons chopped onion

1 teaspoon salt

½ teaspoon pepper

6 egg whites

2 cups cooked chestnuts, chopped

¼ cup melted butter

Hard-boiled eggs, to garnish

Add onion, salt, pepper and egg whites to spinach. Beat together with wire whip until smooth. Have ready a 3-pint mold ring greased with butter. Fill mold with spinach mixture and bake in 375° oven for 20 minutes. Remove from mold and turn out on platter. Fill center with chestnuts and melted butter. Surround with hard-boiled eggs cut in quarters. Serves 12.

3

The Keys GOURMETS flock to enjoy meals at this smart supper club, under the direction of Miss Mary Helen Gray.

Dinner, 6:00 p.m. to 11:00 p.m., except Sunday.

NUT AND HONEY TORTE

1 cup zwieback crumbs, crushed
1 cup pecans or walnuts, chopped
1 teaspoon baking powder
¼ teaspoon cinnamon
¼ teaspoon salt
1 teaspoon vanilla
3 eggs, separated
½ cup sugar

Mix dry ingredients (except sugar). Add vanilla. Beat egg yolks until light, add sugar and beat again until a light lemon color. Add to dry ingredients, mixing thoroughly. Beat egg whites until stiff and fold into mixture. Pour into greased pan, 8 x 12 inches. Bake in 325° oven for ½ hour.

SYRUP

Combine 2 cups water, ½ cup honey and 1 cup sugar and boil for 30 minutes. Pour syrup slowly over hot torte so it will be completely absorbed. Let stand 6 hours. Serves 12.

PAINTING BY EDITH HARPER

Corner Cupboard THIS restaurant, operated by Mr. and Mrs. William Hoffman, was once an old log home.

Lunch, dinner, 11:30 a.m. to 8:00 p.m. Closed Monday and from October 25 to April 21.

BREAD

Add 2 tablespoons sugar and 1½ teaspoons salt to 2 cups scalded milk, cool to lukewarm. Crumble 2 cakes yeast in a large mixing bowl, add ¼ cup water. Stir until yeast is dissolved, then blend in warm milk mixture. Sift in 4 cups of flour, stirring to smoothness. Add 3 tablespoons melted shortening and 2 more cups of flour. Stir until dough leaves the sides of the mixing bowl. Turn dough out on a lightly floured board, knead until smooth, elastic and bubbled under surface (5 to 8 minutes). Roll dough into a ball and place in greased mixing bowl. Cover with dry cloth, put in warm place and let rise to double its bulk. Divide dough into 2 equal parts. Knead each one for a minute or two before shaping into loaf form. Put each into a greased loaf pan, brush tops with melted butter. Cover loaves; set in warm place until they are double in bulk. Bake in 400° preheated oven for 15 minutes, then in 350° oven for about 40 minutes.

PAINTING BY CHARLES W. MOSS

Pritchett's Smörgåsbord

AT THIS modern restaurant, you can sample over 50 dishes on the smörgåsbord table to whet your appetite for the main course.

Lunch, dinner, noon to 9:00 p.m., except Monday.

HERRING SALAD

3 cups pickled herring, diced
1½ cups boiled potatoes, diced
1½ cups pickled beets, diced
½ cup apples, diced
¼ cup onion, chopped
⅓ cup pickled gherkins, diced
4 tablespoons vinegar
2 tablespoons water
2 tablespoons sugar

White pepper, to taste
1 pint sour cream, beaten stiff

Thoroughly mix herring, potatoes, beets, apples, onion and gherkins. Blend vinegar, water, sugar and pepper before adding to herring mixture; toss gently. When ready to serve pour sour cream over top and garnish with hard-boiled eggs and parsley.

U. S. 20 at State Highway 112, Elkhart, Indiana

NORTH CENTRAL 3
145

Stock Yard Inn

LOCATED in Chicago's famous stockyards, this inn has been catering to cattlemen and meat lovers for decades. In the Sirloin Room you may select your own steak, "brand" it, and then wait for it to be cooked to your taste. Overnight accommodations.

Lunch, dinner daily. Reservations necessary.

MARINATED BEEF SLICES

  1-pound sirloin steak, cooked
  1 onion, sliced
    Salt and pepper
  1 ounce lemon juice
  1 cup sour cream
    Lettuce

Slice cooked sirloin into julienne strips. Add sliced onion and salt and pepper, to taste. Sprinkle lemon juice over meat mixture and blend in sour cream. Mix well and serve on lettuce leaf. This is fast replacing shrimp cocktail as the most popular appetizer here.

3

NORTH CENTRAL
146

4178 South Halsted Street, Chicago, Illinois

The Imperial House FINE food and elegant surroundings have made this distinguished restaurant a favorite with Chicago's gourmets and out-of-town visitors.

Lunch, dinner. Dinner only Sunday, from 4:30 p.m. on. Reservations preferred.

ZABAGLIONE FOR TWO

    3 egg yolks
4½ teaspoons sugar
1½ ounces dry, white wine
1½ ounces Marsala or sherry wine
    ½ ounce brandy
    Nutmeg
    Whipped cream

Mix egg yolks with sugar, wines and brandy. Pour the whole mixture into a narrow double boiler. (Water in double boiler at 90° to 100° F.). Whip until 4 times its former size. Serve in ice-cream dishes and sprinkle with nutmeg and a dash of whipped cream. A truly festive holiday dessert.

50 East Walton Place, Chicago, Illinois

PAINTING BY LILLIAN SCALZO

New Salem Lodge

THIS establishment is located at the entrance to New Salem State Park and the restored Lincoln village. Overnight accommodations and vacation facilities. Reservations advisable.

Breakfast, lunch, dinner daily. Open March 15 to November 15.

FRUIT ICEBOX CAKE

2 cups milk

1 pound marshmallows

1 cup whipping cream

1 teaspoon vanilla

1 No. 2 can pineapple tidbits, drained

½ cup nutmeats, chopped

2 cups graham cracker crumbs

Bring milk to boil in a double boiler. Add marshmallows to milk, stir until melted. Let cool. Whip cream, flavor it with vanilla, then fold into marshmallow mixture. Add pineapple and nutmeats. Sprinkle an oblong dish with graham cracker crumbs, then pour mixture over it. Top with another layer of crumbs. Chill overnight. It may be served plain or topped with whipped cream. Serves 12.

3

NORTH CENTRAL

148

New Salem State Park, Petersburg, Illinois

Southern Air VENETTE HULLETT is the owner and manager of this eating place, which is noted for its fine Southern cuisine and the beautiful gardens surrounding it.

Dinner, 5:00 p.m. to 8:00 p.m.; Sunday, noon to 8:00 p.m. Closed Monday and January 2 to February 1.

FRESH VEGETABLE CASSEROLE

8 small new potatoes
8 baby carrots
1 small cauliflower, break in
    flowerlets
1 cup fresh peas
1 cup baby lima beans
½ pound process cheese, sliced
2 cups medium cream sauce
    Several celery stalks and onions
1 tablespoon cheese, grated

Cook vegetables separately (except celery and onions). Drain well; place in casserole. Add sliced cheese to hot cream sauce and stir until melted. Chop a few stalks of celery and a couple of small onions together and add water to them. Simmer until a broth is obtained. Mix this broth into sauce and pour over vegetables. Place casserole in 350° oven, about 30 minutes, until well heated. Sprinkle with grated cheese and garnish with parsley. Serves 8.

3045 Clearlake Avenue, Springfield, Illinois

NORTH CENTRAL 3

PAINTING BY CHESTER BRATTEN

Old Spinning Wheel TWENTY-FIVE acres of
flower gardens surround this restaurant, which is located in a
reproduction of an Early American log cabin.

*Lunch, noon to 3:00 p.m.; dinner, 5:00 p.m. to 8:00 p.m. Closed Monday and
during January.*

MINT PIE

FILLING

    ¼ pound butter
    1 cup powdered sugar
    2 eggs
    2 squares unsweetened chocolate
    ¼ teaspoon essence of peppermint

Cream butter and sugar together until smooth. Beat eggs in one at a time until mixture is fluffy. Mix in melted chocolate and peppermint.

CRUST

Roll 14 graham crackers very fine and mix with ¼ pound butter. Line pie tin and bake 20 minutes in 350° oven. Cool and fill crust with mint filling. Top with whipped cream before serving.

3

NORTH CENTRAL
150

421 East Ogden Avenue, Hinsdale, Illinois

Nielsen's Restaurant

VIKING murals adorn the walls of this friendly Danish restaurant. Hans Nielsen is the owner and manager here.

Lunch, dinner, after-theater supper daily. Reservations necessary for large groups.

FRIKADELLER

1½ pounds ground steak
½ pound ground pork
1 onion, grated
3 to 4 slices white bread
Milk or cream
⅛ teaspoon pepper
4 tablespoons flour
¼ teaspoon cloves
1½ teaspoons salt
2 eggs
Shortening and hot fat

Grind meat 3 or 4 times. Add onion and bread softened in milk. Mix well. Add remaining ingredients (except shortening and fat). Use milk or cream to hold mixture and form into meat balls. Put shortening in pan to heat. Place each meat ball in pan with a spoon which has been dipped in hot fat and fry till light brown. Make gravy by adding more liquid to the pan gravy; thicken with mixture of flour and milk or cream.

7840 South Western Avenue, Chicago, Illinois

NORTH CENTRAL 3

The Wagon Wheel FORMERLY a three-table truck stop, this establishment today offers overnight accommodations and vacation facilities. Reservations advisable.

Lunch, dinner daily.

LUSCH TORTE

For this recipe you will need: ½ pound vanilla wafers, 1 cup broken pecans, 1 pound confectioners' sugar, ½ pound butter, 6 egg yolks, 4 egg whites, salt and vanilla to taste. Crush wafers into crumbs, save ¼ cup crumbs to top torte. Add to remaining crumbs, 2 tablespoons pecans, 2 tablespoons sugar and enough butter to hold mixture together. Press into the bottom of 1½-inch-deep pan, 8 inches square. Bake at 300° until browned, then cool. Save ½ cup sugar for meringue. Then take part of remaining sugar and the butter and put into mixer. Start at slow speed and increase to fast. Add remaining sugar and whip. Add yolks, one at a time, and whip. Add salt and vanilla. Fold in pecans. Make meringue of egg whites and ½ cup sugar and fold into butter mixture. Place over crust and top with crumbs. Cover with wax paper and freeze for 12 hours. Serve with whipped cream. Serves 12.

PAINTING BY JAMES F. HEINLEN

Ridgeland Farm

THIS restaurant is noted for its chicken, steak, chop, and roast-beef dinners served in a pleasant rustic atmosphere.

Dinner, 5:00 p.m. to midnight weekdays; week ends, noon to midnight. Reservations advised on week ends.

APPLE PIE

CRUST

2 cups flour
1 teaspoon salt
1 teaspoon sugar
⅔ cup lard
4 tablespoons ice water

Combine flour, salt and sugar. Blend in lard and water and mix together until none sticks to the bowl. Press into a ball and roll out into 2 crusts.

FILLING

4 to 5 apples, sliced thin
1 teaspoon cinnamon
Few pieces of butter
¾ to 1 cup sugar

Mix together and put in crust-lined tin. Cover with top crust and bake 15 minutes at 400° and 30 minutes at 350°.

110th and Ridgeland Avenues, Worth, Illinois   **NORTH CENTRAL 3**

Mill Race Inn   IN SUMMER, meals are served on an outdoor terrace and gallery over the mill race.

Lunch, dinner. Closed Monday, Decoration Day, Fourth of July, and November 15 to April 1.

FRESH MUSHROOMS AND CHICKEN LIVERS ON WILD RICE

1 cup wild rice
4 cups water
1 pound mushrooms
1 pound chicken livers
¼ cup butter
4 tablespoons flour
2 cups chicken broth
½ teaspoon salt
¼ teaspoon pepper
¼ cup sherry wine

Boil rice briskly in water 30 or 40 minutes. Do not stir. Drain off water and steam until dry and fluffy. Sauté mushrooms and chicken livers in butter. Sprinkle with flour and mix well. Add chicken broth and cook until thickened. Season with salt and pepper. Add sherry. Serve over wild rice.

3

NORTH CENTRAL
154

4 East State Street, Geneva, Illinois

Osthoff's

THIS summer resort has been owned by the same family for over 65 years. Overnight accommodations.

Breakfast, lunch, dinner. Closed September 15 to June 15.

SWEET-SOUR FISH

Fillet a 3-pound lake trout. Boil fish bones, head and tail with 1 sliced onion; ⅓ cup vinegar; ⅓ cup sugar; pinch of salt; 2 sliced celery stalks; 2 sliced carrots; 1 spray dill; 2 bay leaves; 3 cloves; ¼ teaspoon allspice and a ½ sliced lemon. Add enough water to cover ingredients. To keep broth clear, boil very slowly for 20 minutes and then strain. Cut fish fillets in 3-inch pieces and place in strained broth. Boil slowly until fish is done—about 15 minutes.

Place 1½ cups fish broth in a sauce pan and add 3 sliced onions; ½ sliced lemon; 1 cup washed raisins; ⅓ cup vinegar and a ⅓ cup sugar. Boil until onions are clear. Add 1 teaspoon cornstarch mixed with water and boil until clear. Cool. Remove fish from broth and place in glass dish, pour raisin sauce over fish and let jell. Sprinkle with parsley and chopped chives. Serve with sliced tomatoes, cucumbers and lemon on crisp lettuce. Makes 6 portions.

Off State Highway 57, Elkhart Lake, Wisconsin

NORTH CENTRAL **3**

The Flame

TWENTY-ONE years ago this restaurant was a barbecue stand; today, it occupies an elegant modern building with several dining rooms. Huge picture windows enable diners to view the Aerial Bridge and the harbor.

Lunch, dinner, except Sunday.

CHICKEN À LA KIEV

Remove the skin from the breast of a 3½-pound chicken. Split the breast and remove breastbone. Leave wing bones on. Flatten chicken out with an old-fashioned wooden potato masher so that it is perfectly flat. Place ⅛-pound butter in the center of the breast and wrap the meat around it, leaving the wing bones extented. Dip into egg and milk mixture, then drop into cracker crumbs. This process seals in the butter. Drop the chicken breast into deep fat until it turns a golden brown. Take out of hot fat and put into 350° oven for about 12 minutes. Place chop holder on wing bones. Serve on lettuce leaf with a half peach. (Beware of squirting butter when you cut into chicken!)

3

NORTH CENTRAL   *353 South Fifth Avenue, West, Duluth, Minnesota*

Hotel Anderson THREE generations of Anderson cooks have made this hotel famous. Overnight accommodations and vacation facilities.

Breakfast, lunch, dinner. Closed Saturday and Sunday evenings December 1 to March 1.

CEDRIC ADAMS CAKE

4 squares chocolate, melted
4 tablespoons butter, melted
2 cups sugar
2 teaspoons soda
2 cups rich milk
3 cups flour, sifted
¼ teaspoon cream of tartar
¼ teaspoon salt
2 teaspoons vanilla
4 egg whites, beaten stiff

Add sugar to combined chocolate and butter. Dissolve soda in milk, then add dry ingredients and milk alternately to the chocolate mixture. Add vanilla and fold in egg whites. Pour batter into three 9-inch greased layer pans. Bake in 350° oven for 20 to 25 minutes. When cool, frost lavishly with 7-minute icing and drip melted chocolate over frosting after it is set.

Four blocks from U. S. 61, Wabasha, Minnesota

The Bungalow Inn

MUSIC and entertainment are featured here in addition to excellent food. Elmer Hartwig is the owner of this distinguished eating place, which has two large dining rooms. The one that is illustrated is done in a striking zebra motif.

Lunch, dinner until midnight, except Sunday.

FRENCH DRESSING

1 10-ounce can tomato soup
¾ cup vinegar
2 tablespoons finely ground onion
1 teaspoon Worcestershire sauce
1 teaspoon celery salt
1 teaspoon dry mustard
1 cup Mazola oil
1 teaspoon paprika
¾ cup sugar

Blend all ingredients in a jar and shake violently before serving. Remainder of dressing can be stored in the refrigerator. Try it on a tossed salad as it's served here with French fried butterfly shrimp.

3

NORTH CENTRAL *6221 Fifty-sixth Avenue N., Minneapolis, Minnesota*
158

PAINTING BY JAMES F. HEINLEN

Eibner's

TRAVELERS stopping at Alois Eibner's eating place will find it hard to believe that this community was nearly wiped out by a Sioux uprising less than 90 years ago.

Breakfast, lunch, dinner, 6:30 a.m. to midnight. Closed Monday.

DATE-NUT TORTE

4 eggs, beaten
1 cup sugar
1 cup bread crumbs, dry
1 teaspoon baking powder
½ teaspoon salt
1 teaspoon vanilla
12 ounces dates, chopped
1 cup walnuts, chopped
Whipped cream

Slowly add sugar to eggs and beat until thick and lemon-colored. Mix bread crumbs with baking powder and salt and fold carefully into egg mixture. Add vanilla and spread in a well-greased and floured pan. Sprinkle with dates and walnuts. Bake in a 325° oven for 45 to 60 minutes. Serve in squares topped with whipped cream.

108 North Minnesota Street, New Ulm, Minnesota   **NORTH CENTRAL** **3**

Hot Fish Shop

HERE, at the foot of Sugar Loaf Hill, is a restaurant which offers patrons nearly every variety of fresh-water fish, cooked or to take out.

Lunch, dinner, 11:30 a.m. to 8:30 p.m. Closed Monday and from Thanksgiving Day to January 1.

PICKLED FRESH-WATER FISH

If you catch more fresh-water fish (fat fish are best) than you can immediately use, you can preserve them a week or more by pickling. Cut larger fish in chunks; cover with salt overnight. Then rinse fish in cold water and put in kettle. Season with bay leaf and a few whole allspice; cover with equal mixture of vinegar and water. Add 1 or 2 onions according to your taste. Boil on slow fire for 15 to 25 minutes, depending on the size of the fish chunks, and set aside to cool. The juice will jell and preserve the fish for a week or two under refrigeration. True fish lovers will enjoy this pickled fish with any meal.

3

NORTH CENTRAL
160

South Mankato Avenue, Winona, Minnesota

PAINTING BY JAMES F. HEINLEN

Carroll's White House   GERTRUDE AND

RUSSELL CARROLL are owners of this 75-year-old inn over-looking Lake Shady. All of the restaurant's fruits and vege-tables are grown in the adjoining garden.

Dinner, 5:00 to 8:30 p.m. weekdays; Sunday, 12:30 p.m. to 8:30 p.m. Closed January 2 to Easter.

APPLE TORTE

1 egg
¾ cup sugar
¾ cup apples, sliced
1 teaspoon baking powder
½ cup flour
Pinch salt
¼ teaspoon almond extract
¼ cup walnut meats, chopped
Whipped cream

Beat egg lightly, add sugar and apple slices. Then stir in remaining ingredients (except cream). Mix well. Pour into greased pie tin and bake in 325° oven for 25 minutes. Serve topped with whipped cream.

U. S. 52, north of Rochester, Oronoco, Minnesota   **NORTH CENTRAL 3**

The Oaks A REPUTATION for outstanding food, prepared under the direction of Chef Walter Kelly, brings diners from a hundred-mile radius. Overnight accommodations and complete vacation facilities.

Lunch, dinner daily.

REX TURKEY VIENNESE

> 1 broiler turkey, 4 to 5 pounds
> Salt and pepper, to taste
> 3 tablespoons flour, plus enough
>   to roll turkey in
> ¼ pound butter
> 1 tablespoon paprika
> 1½ cups stock
> 1 quart sour cream

Disjoint turkey, season with salt and pepper. Roll in flour. Heat butter in pan and sauté turkey to a golden brown. Put in 350° oven and bake for about 30 minutes or until tender. Remove turkey from pan, add flour and paprika and fry for a few minutes, stirring often. Add stock, stirring briskly. Add sour cream. Bring to a boil, then strain and pour over turkey or serve on the side with wild rice or buttered egg noodles. Serves 6 to 8.

Off U. S. 61 to Minnesota City, Minnesota

Steinhart Park Lodge NEAR Arbor Lodge
State Park, this restaurant lies in a truly sylvan setting.

Special luncheons for groups; dinner. Closed Monday and January 1 to April 1.
Reservations advisable.

SPECIAL POTATOES

Select smooth 8- to 10-ounce baking potatoes. Scrub well. Pierce each end. Place on end in a pressure cooker with customary small amount of water. Hold pressure at about 10 pounds. Test after 20 minutes with toothpick. When done let cool at room temperature. Potatoes may be held in refrigerator several days. When ready to serve, place in deep fat (300° to 325°) for 8 to 12 minutes depending on whether potatoes are at room temperature or chilled. Take potatoes from deep fat and wrap in paper towel, pressing gently to soften. Open with fork prongs, fluff up potato. Top with pat of butter and dash of paprika. These unusual potatoes are a specialty of the managers, Mr. and Mrs. George Carpenter.

The Derby Cafe

HERE is a hunters' paradise—an eating and overnight spot in bird-hunting territory.

Breakfast, lunch, dinner until 11:00 p.m. Closed December 1 to May 1.

SOPHIE DERBY'S STRAWBERRY CREAM PIE

    1 pint milk
    ⅓ cup sugar
    3 egg yolks
    4 tablespoons cornstarch
    1½ teaspoons vanilla
    1 pint fresh whole strawberries
    1 9-inch pie shell, baked

Heat milk and sugar together in a double boiler. Beat yolks well and add cornstarch to them and beat again. Add this to the milk mixture and cook until thick. (It can even be beaten while cooking.) Add vanilla and chill. Line baked pie shell with sliced berries and pour cream mixture into shell.

MERINGUE TOPPING

For topping you will need: 2 egg whites, a dash of salt, 1 cup fresh, crushed strawberries, 1½ cups sugar.

Beat egg whites until frothy, then add salt. Fold in crushed berries and gradually add sugar. Beat until thick and fluffy. Spread over pie, which should be chilled before serving.

3

NORTH CENTRAL

204 Main Street, Chamberlain, South Dakota

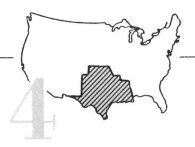

SOUTH CENTRAL

The Ozark and farm country, where good food is simply prepared, are famous for such dishes as country-smoked ham, milk gravy, fried chicken, persimmon pudding, peach cobbler, and homemade ice cream. In sharp contrast is the exotic Creole cuisine of the Gulf coast and the highly seasoned Mexican favorites so popular in southern Texas.

Medart's

THE Olde Cheshire room here is furnished with beautiful antiques and has a fireplace.

Breakfast, lunch, dinner, 7:00 a.m. to 1:30 a.m. daily.

STEAK AND KIDNEY PIE

    1 pound round steak, diced
    2 beef kidneys, diced
    1 small onion, diced
    ½ cup flour
      Salt and pepper, to taste
    1 tablespoon Lea and Perrins
      sauce
    1 teaspoon Tabasco sauce
    1½ tablespoons Kitchen Bouquet

Put kidneys and onion in stew pan with water to cover. Boil until tender. Stir in flour mixed with a little water, until smooth. Add remaining seasonings and steak last. Cook until tender. Place in individual casseroles.

PASTRY

Combine as for biscuits, 1 cup shortening, 2½ cups flour, ½ teaspoon salt, 2½ teaspoons baking powder, and ½ cup milk. Pat dough out to about ½ inch thick and cover the casseroles. Brush the top with 1 beaten egg and 1 tablespoon cream combined. Bake in oven until brown. Serves 4.

SOUTH CENTRAL   *7036 Clayton Avenue (U. S. 40), St. Louis, Missouri*

PAINTING BY BILL RAKOCY

Old Plantation KARL AND VERA KIEKERT own
this stately eating place, located in a lovely old home which
was built in 1849 and is furnished with antiques.

*Dinner, 5:30 p.m. to 8:30 p.m. weekdays; Sunday, 12:30 p.m. to 8:00 p.m. Closed
Wednesday.*

ORANGE ICEBOX DESSERT

⅔ cup sugar

3 egg yolks, beaten

½ cup orange juice

2 tablespoons lemon juice

1 teaspoon grated orange peel

⅛ teaspoon salt

3 egg whites, beaten stiff

1 cup chilled canned milk, whipped

2 cups vanilla wafer crumbs

Gradually add sugar to egg yolks and
beat thoroughly. Add fruit juices, orange peel and salt. Fold in egg whites
and whipped milk. Pour into refrigerator tray lined with wafer crumbs. Sprinkle top with crumbs and freeze firm.
Serves 8 to 10 people.

9802 East U. S. 40, Kansas City, Missouri

SOUTH CENTRAL 4

Kentwood Arms Hotel   HERE, among land-
scaped grounds, is a serene overnight spot on the highway.

Breakfast, lunch, dinner daily.

OZARK BLACK WALNUT CHOCOLATE TORTE

½ cup black walnuts, chopped
½ cup chocolate cookie crumbs
1 envelope plain gelatin
¼ cup cold water
1 package semi-sweet chocolate
½ cup sugar
¼ teaspoon salt
½ cup milk
3 eggs, separated
1 cup cream, whipped

Combine crumbs and nuts. Rinse out one 8-inch spring form pan with cold water. Line with wax paper. Cover bottom with half of crumb mixture. Soften gelatin in water. Cook chocolate, ¼ cup sugar, salt and milk in a double boiler until blended. Beat egg yolks and add hot mixture slowly, stirring rapidly. Return to double boiler; cook, stirring, till thickened. Remove; add gelatin, stir until dissolved. Chill until nearly thickened. Beat egg whites and add ¼ cup sugar. Fold in chocolate mixture and cream. Turn into pan. Top with remaining crumb mixture. Chill till firm.

4

SOUTH CENTRAL

U. S. 66, Springfield, Missouri

PAINTING BY JESSE BEARD RICKLY

French-American Inn

GUESTS may visit the actual trading post on the inn grounds where the French bartered with the Indians long ago in pioneer days.

Lunch, noon to 2:00 p.m.; dinner, 5:00 to 7:00 p.m.; Sunday dinner, noon to 7:00 p.m. Closed Friday evening and December 1 to April 1.

PERSIMMON PUDDING

1½ quarts of persimmons
2 eggs, well beaten
¾ cup honey
1 pint milk
½ cup butter
Ground cinnamon and nutmeg, to taste
Flour

Mash and rub persimmons through a coarse sieve or fine colander. To this add eggs, honey, milk, butter cut in small pieces, seasoning and enough flour to make batter stiff. Bake in 350° oven for 30 minutes.

Second and Merchant, Ste. Genevieve, Missouri

SOUTH CENTRAL 4

PAINTING BY LORA E. ADKINS

Sherman House LOCATED in a pleasant old home, this establishment offers travelers comfortable overnight accommodations as well as excellent meals.

Breakfast, lunch, dinner daily.

PEACH COBBLER

CRUST

Combine 2¼ cups sifted flour, 1 teaspoon salt, ¾ cup Crisco, and ¼ cup water. Line a deep dish with crust, reserving enough for top strips.

FILLING

    4 cups peaches, sliced
    2 cups peach juice
    1 cup sugar
    2 tablespoons cornstarch
    2 tablespoons butter
    1 tablespoon lemon juice

Combine sugar, cornstarch and butter with peach juice. Cook until thick, about 5 minutes. Pour over peaches and add lemon juice. Pour into crust-lined pan. Dot with butter. Top with crust strips, and bake in 325° oven for 30 minutes. Serves 15.

4

SOUTH CENTRAL
170

Main and First Streets, Gideon, Missouri

McDonald Tea Room THIS restaurant was started by Mrs. Virginia McDonald in one room of a remodeled blacksmith shop. The popularity of Mrs. McDonald's home cooking made it necessary to enlarge the building.

Lunch, dinner daily.

SPAGHETTI LOAF

    1 cup spaghetti, cooked
    2 tablespoons butter, melted
    3 eggs, beaten
    1 teaspoon salt
      Pepper to taste
    1 green pepper, chopped
1¼ cups cheese, grated
    2 pimentos, chopped
    1 tablespoon parsley, chopped

    1 cup milk
    1 cup thick white sauce

Mix butter with beaten eggs; add salt, pepper, green pepper, one cup of cheese, pimentos, parsley and milk. Combine with spaghetti and bake in a loaf pan for 45 minutes at 300°. Turn out on serving dish and "ice" with white sauce combined with remaining quarter cup of cheese.

State Highways 6 and 13, Gallatin, Missouri

SOUTH CENTRAL 4

PAINTING BY LOUIS FREUND

Riverside Inn

THERE are large patios, surrounded by gardens, for outdoor dining at this restaurant, which is located at a bend on the Finley River.

Luncheons by appointment only. Dinner daily.

CAESAR SALAD

- 1 head romaine
- 1 cup croutons
- 1 lemon
- 2 tablespoons Parmesan cheese
- ¼ teaspoon black pepper
- 1 warm egg

Cut romaine into ½-inch strips; put into salad bowl. Add croutons. Squeeze lemon over this, then add cheese and pepper. Break egg into salad and toss well. Then add chilled dressing (see below) and toss again.

CHILLED DRESSING

- 8 anchovy fillets
  Dash of Lea and Perrins sauce
- ¼ teaspoon hot mustard
- 5 ounces olive oil with garlic
- 3 ounces wine vinegar

Place a bowl in large pan of crushed ice. Chop anchovies to paste. Add remaining ingredients, mix well and leave in ice to chill.

4

SOUTH CENTRAL
172

On U. S. 65, 1½ miles northeast of Ozark, Missouri

Hotel Arkansas

THE CHARMING rustic dining room called The Orchard is in a wing of this hotel. Overnight accommodations; vacation facilities.

Breakfast, lunch, dinner daily.

MEAT LOAF

1 pound each: ground veal, beef, and pork
2 eggs
⅓ cup onion, chopped
2 teaspoons salt
¼ teaspoon dry mustard
⅛ teaspoon seasoning salt (optional)
⅛ teaspoon celery salt
⅛ teaspoon paprika
¼ teaspoon black pepper

Have meat ground only once in a food chopper with a coarse blade. Combine meats thoroughly in a large mixing bowl. Beat eggs well, add onion and other seasonings and mix again. Combine with meat and stir or knead until blended. Pack into an oiled glass bread loaf pan and unmold onto a flat baking pan. Bake in a 350° oven for 1½ hours or until well done. Serves 20. This is perfect for a party or recipe may be halved for family meals. Good cold.

Second and Poplar, Rogers, Arkansas

SOUTH CENTRAL 4

Bruno's Little Italy

CANDLELIGHT and red-checkered tablecloths are a perfect setting for the authentic Italian foods served here.

Lunch, dinner, noon to 9:00 p.m.; Saturday, noon to 11:00 p.m. Closed Tuesday and during Christmas holidays.

VEAL CUTLET À LA PARMIGIANA

1 pound baby veal (4 slices)
Salt and pepper, to taste
8 ounces flour
1 egg
1 jigger cream
1 cup cracker meal
Deep fat
2 cans Hunt's tomato sauce
1 shaker grated Parmesan cheese
½ pound American or mozzarelli cheese

Season veal slices and roll in flour, then in a combination of beaten egg and cream. Dredge in cracker meal. Fry in deep fat until brown and drain. Place in individual casseroles and cover with heated tomato sauce and grated cheese. Top with strips of solid cheese. Sprinkle with parsley and pimento and bake in 450° oven for 10 minutes.

4

SOUTH CENTRAL

3400 West Roosevelt Road, Little Rock, Arkansas

174

Shadow Hill Tea Room   MRS. GEORGE
HOLMES owns and manages this tea room, which is housed in a romantic old Mississippi home.

Lunch, dinner, except Tuesday and Christmas Day. Reservations necessary.

FRIED CUSTARD

Put 1 quart milk in double boiler with ¼ teaspoon soda (to keep milk from curdling), and 3 sticks cinnamon. Let come almost to a boil. Take 1 cup warm milk from pan and stir into 2 tablespoons flour and 4 tablespoons cornstarch. Beat till smooth. To this mixture, add another cup warm milk from double boiler, 1 cup sugar, and 6 egg yolks. Beat well; then combine with rest of milk in double boiler. Stir till mixture thickens. Remove from stove, add a pinch of salt, 1 teaspoon vanilla, and 1 tablespoon butter. Beat thoroughly. Pour into greased 8-inch cake pan about ¾ inch thick. Cool and place in refrigerator overnight. Cut into squares. Beat 3 egg whites well. Dip custard into whites, then into finely ground cracker meal. Fry in hot grease, 1 inch deep, till brown. Drain on paper. Serve hot. Serves 8.

Off U. S. 51, Hernando, Mississippi

SOUTH CENTRAL 4

PAINTING BY ADOLPH KRONENGOLD

Trilby's Teddy and Trilby Steimer's restaurant, located in a lovely old mansion, specializes in seafoods.

Lunch, dinner, except Sunday. Closed last two weeks of December. Reservations at height of season.

CHRISTMAS PIE

CRUST

Combine 1½ cups finely ground Brazil nutmeats with ½ teaspoon sugar. Press this mixture to sides and bottom of 9-inch pie tin. Bake in 400° oven for 8 minutes or until lightly browned.

FILLING

Soak 1 envelope of gelatin in ¼ cup of water. Beat 3 egg yolks with fork and add ¼ cup sugar and ⅛ teaspoon salt.

Gradually stir in 1½ cups scalded milk. Cook in double boiler over hot, not boiling, water till mixture coats spoon. Remove from fire and stir in gelatin. Chill custard till thickened. Beat till smooth. Add 1½ cups thinly sliced cherries, 3 tablespoons rum or rum flavoring. Beat 3 egg whites. Then add ¼ cup sugar, continuing to beat till whites are stiff. Fold into custard; pour into crust. Top with whipped cream.

SOUTH CENTRAL

4

176

U. S. 90, Ocean Springs, Mississippi

PAINTING BY ADOLPH KRONENGOLD

Friendship House

THIS establishment is a handy stop for tourists because it is open every day. Overnight accommodations. Reservations suggested.

Breakfast, lunch, dinner, 7:00 a.m. to midnight daily.

CHOCOLATE PIE

1½ cups sugar
½ cup cornstarch
½ cup cocoa
¼ teaspoon salt
2½ cups milk
3 egg yolks
½ teaspoon vanilla
1 cooked pie shell
Whipped cream to cover

Mix sugar, cornstarch, cocoa and salt together. Then add ½ cup of milk and egg yolks. Blend these ingredients. Add remaining two cups of milk. Heat mixture in double boiler, stirring occasionally until mixture becomes thick. Add vanilla. Cool, then pour into baked pie shell. Top with whipped cream.

On U. S. 90, Mississippi City, Mississippi

SOUTH CENTRAL 4

Court of Two Sisters

THIS restaurant is located in a building which was erected in 1832 and was once the home of the Governor. Meals served in a cool garden.

Breakfast, lunch, dinner daily.

SHRIMP AU GRATIN

2 pounds shrimp
Dash of lemon juice
½ cup butter or oleo
1 cup flour
1 teaspoon salt
¼ teaspoon pepper
3 egg yolks
2 tablespoons sherry wine
2 tablespoons grated cheese
Bread crumbs

Clean and wash shrimp. Place in saucepan with a quart of water and a dash of lemon juice, then bring to a boil for 10 minutes. In another pan melt butter or oleo, then add flour and stir till smooth. Then add 4 cups shrimp stock, stirring constantly. Stir in seasonings, yolks, wine, cheese. Add shrimp; top with crumbs and more cheese. Bake in buttered casserole at 350° to 375° about 15 minutes. Serves 6 to 8.

4 SOUTH CENTRAL

613 Royal Street, New Orleans, Louisiana

The Coffee Pot

THIS restaurant is surrounded by some of the oldest and most historic buildings in the famous French Quarter of New Orleans.

Breakfast, lunch, 7:30 a.m. to 8:00 p.m., except Sunday.

LITTLE RICE CAKES

1 cup boiled cold rice
3 whole eggs
½ cup granulated sugar
½ teaspoon salt
Pinch nutmeg
1 cup flour
3 teaspoons baking powder
Hot fat for frying
Powdered sugar and cinnamon

Beat eggs until fluffy; add other ingredients (except fat and cinnamon mixture). Beat well. Drop by tablespoonfuls into hot fat, and fry to a golden brown. Drain on brown paper and sprinkle with powdered sugar and cinnamon. Here these cakes are served with apple jelly or Louisiana orange marmalade as an added treat with a chicken or ham dinner. This recipe serves 6.

710 St. Peter Street, New Orleans, Louisiana

SOUTH CENTRAL 4

Commander's Palace FRANK MORAN owns
this restaurant in the garden district of New Orleans.

Lunch, dinner, 11:00 a.m. to midnight. Reservations necessary.

REMOULADE SAUCE

2 eggs
4 tablespoons paprika
2 teaspoons salt
½ cup Creole mustard
1½ pints vegetable oil
½ cup vinegar
1 lemon
½ cup each, shallots and celery
3 cloves garlic, crushed
2 stalks parsley
¼ cup tomato catsup

3 bay leaves
2 tablespoons horseradish
Tabasco sauce, to taste

Put eggs, paprika, salt, and Creole mustard into a mixing bowl. Add oil slowly; after mixture is thick, add vinegar. Grate lemon rind into mixture, then quarter lemon and squeeze in juice. Finely chop celery, garlic, parsley and shallots, add to mixture. Blend in catsup, bay leaves, horseradish and Tabasco. Chill for 6 hours. Serve with cold fish or meat. Makes 1½ quarts.

SOUTH CENTRAL *1403 Washington Avenue, New Orleans, Louisiana*

4

180

Patio Royal

LOCATED in the French Quarter this eating place is on a street lined with historic old homes and gardens. One modern note in this converted Creole mansion is the air-conditioned outdoor dining and dancing patio.

Breakfast, lunch, dinner from 8:00 a.m. to 1:00 a.m. daily.

CRAB MEAT BAR-NONE

1 cup lump crab meat
1 small shallot, chopped fine
1 tablespoon mushrooms, pieces
1 tablespoon butter
  Salt to taste
1 peppercorn, crushed
1 ounce sherry wine
  Toast points
½ cup Hollandaise sauce

Sauté shallot and mushroom pieces in butter for about 3 minutes. Then add crab meat and sauté for several minutes. Add salt and peppercorn. Stir in wine a minute before taking mixture from fire. Mold mixture in a teacup and turn out on trimmed toast. Top with Hollandaise. This makes 1 serving.

417 Royal Street, New Orleans, Louisiana

Madeline's Restaurant OWNED and managed by Madeline Bigelow, this eating place is extremely popular with residents of Houston who enjoy the fine French food. Specialties are cheesecake and seafood and meat dishes.

Dinner, 6:00 p.m. to midnight, except Monday. Reservations on Saturday.

CHOCOLATE FUDGE PIE

1 cup sugar
½ cup butter, melted
2 eggs
⅔ cup flour, sifted
1 square bitter chocolate, melted
1 teaspoon vanilla

Beat sugar and butter together, then add eggs. Beat until thoroughly mixed, add flour and blend well. Add chocolate and vanilla. Pour into a greased pyrex pie plate (no crust) and bake in preheated 325° oven for 25 minutes. Serve with vanilla ice cream. This recipe yields 8 servings.

4218 Montrose Boulevard, Houston, Texas

PAINTING BY KENNETH WEBSTER

Western Hills Hotel THIS establishment has been hailed as a truly modern hotel—a unique combination of the best of city hotel and deluxe motel, with the recreational features of a resort added.

Breakfast, lunch, dinner 24 hours daily.

LEMON BISQUE PIE

2 cups water
1⅛ cups sugar
¼ pound butter
⅓ cup cornstarch
3 eggs
1½ teaspoons salt
2 tablespoons lemon juice
1½ tablespoons unflavored gelatin
1 pint whipping cream
2 baked pie shells
Graham cracker crumbs

Mix 1½ cups water with sugar and butter; bring to a boil. Add ½ cup water, cornstarch, eggs, salt and lemon juice. Dissolve gelatin in a little water and add to custard. Let cool. Whip cream and fold into custard. Pour mixture into pie shells and top with cracker crumbs. Serve warm or chilled.

6451 Camp Bowie Boulevard, Fort Worth, Texas

SOUTH CENTRAL 4

PAINTING BY KENNETH WEBSTER

Town and Country AN interesting decorative scheme makes it easy to pick the "town" or "country" side of this dining room. Whichever side you choose, the food is outstanding and the service is excellent.

Lunch, dinner daily.

CHICKEN WITH YELLOW RICE

1½-pound chicken, whole
1 cup olive oil or shortening
2 green peppers, diced
2 onions, diced
1 pound raw rice
1 quart chicken stock
Salt and pepper, to taste
½ teaspoon saffron
1 tablespoon yellow food color

Heat olive oil in Dutch oven. Fast fry whole chicken. Remove chicken from pan. Braise pepper and onions in same oil for about 10 minutes. Then add rice, chicken stock, seasonings, food color and chicken. Bake in 350° oven for 35 minutes. Serves 4.

4

SOUTH CENTRAL

184

2016 Commerce Street, Dallas, Texas

PAINTING BY HERB SCHIEBOLD

Brookville Hotel

THIS old-fashioned country hotel was established in 1870. Only one main course, fried chicken, is served, but you can have all you want with generous servings of hot biscuits, special coleslaw, and vegetables. Overnight accommodations and vacation facilities.

Evening dinner weekdays; dinner Sunday, at noon and in evening. Closed Monday, Christmas Day, and Thanksgiving Day. Reservations suggested.

OLD-FASHIONED ICE CREAM

4 eggs
2 cups sugar
½ teaspoon salt
3 cups heavy cream
1 tablespoon vanilla
2 quarts whole milk

Beat eggs until very light. Gradually add sugar and salt. Beat mixture well. Then add cream and vanilla. Add milk last. Allow about 2½ inches for swelling in freezer can. Freeze in dasher type old-fashioned ice-cream freezer. Makes 1 gallon of delicious vanilla ice cream.

U. S. 40, west of Salina, Brookville, Kansas

PAINTING BY CHARLES B. WILSON

Pete's Place IN THIS eating place in a rambling old house run by Pete Prichard, you may dine in the kitchen or in one of the 11 dining rooms.

Lunch, dinner, except Tuesday. Closed July 1 to September 1.

ITALIAN MEAT BALLS

1 pound ground meat
2 ounces Parmesan cheese
Salt and black pepper, to taste
½ cup parsley, chopped
½ cup cracker meal
2 eggs
1 can tomato paste
Garlic, to taste

Season ground meat with cheese, salt, parsley and pepper. Add cracker meal; bind mixture with eggs. Make 8 meat balls as large as an egg, flatten them at both ends, and fry them in deep fat or bake them. Then cover them with tomato paste and season with garlic. Simmer until tender. This will be enough for 4 people. Serve with spaghetti.

4 **SOUTH CENTRAL**   *U. S. 270 and State Highway 31, Krebs, Oklahoma*

5

WEST

The best cooking of a dozen nations is to be found in this vast and beautiful area; Mexico, Spain, India, China, the Pacific Islands are but a few. But first in the hearts of the true fan of the wide-open spaces would be a meal of piping-hot round-up stew, served from a real old-fashioned chuck wagon and eaten zestfully under the incredibly blue western sky.

Legend Room

THIS restaurant is operated by the Bon Marché store, a part of Northgate, which is Seattle's 16-million-dollar planned-shopping city. The room was designed by Lionel Pries of the University of Washington. Its murals capture the majesty of the totemic art of six Indian tribes.

Lunch, dinner, except Sunday and Monday. Reservations advisable.

BAKED KIDNEY BEANS

1 pound dry red kidney beans
½ pound salt pork, cut in strips
3 tablespoons onion, chopped
2 tablespoons brown sugar
1 tablespoon dry mustard
2 bay leaves
1 tablespoon cider vinegar
½ clove garlic, minced
2½ tablespoons molasses

Soak beans overnight. Parboil for a half hour. Fry pork until golden brown. Add salt pork and fat with rest of ingredients to beans. Bake in a slow 250° oven for 6 to 7 hours or until tender. Add additional water during baking as needed. Makes 1½ quarts of beans.

5 WEST
188

U. S. 99, Northgate Shopping Center, Seattle, Washington

The Windmill Steak House

ALL the meat and chicken served in the dining rooms here is cooked to order. Sam Harrison is the owner and manager.

Dinner, except Sunday.

SAM'S FAMOUS SALAD DRESSING

1 pint salad dressing
1 egg
1 tablespoon paprika
¼ teaspoon salt
1 quart Wesson oil
1½ teaspoons Worcestershire sauce
1½ teaspoons A-1 sauce
Vinegar, to taste

Whip together salad dressing, egg, paprika and salt. Then slowly add oil, the sauces, and vinegar to taste. Whip about 10 minutes. Keep remaining dressing in refrigerator. This recipe makes 2 quarts of dressing.

U. S. 2 (North Wenatchee Avenue), **Wenatchee, Washington**

PAINTING BY MILDRED NEAL

Log Cabin Inn
OWNED by Anne and Cliff Ruedy, this inn is on the Big Quilcene River. Overnight accommodations and vacation facilities. Reservations preferred.

Breakfast, lunch, dinner. Closed from October 1 to March 1.

ORANGE SNOWFLAKE SALAD

1 cup cottage cheese
1 cup pineapple, shredded
½ cup celery, chopped
1 tablespoon onion, grated
½ cup pineapple juice
2 tablespoons vinegar
½ cup water
Pinch of salt
2 packages orange Jello
¼ teaspoon powdered ginger
2 cups water

Place cottage cheese, pineapple, celery and minced onion in a small loaf pan. Heat pineapple juice, vinegar, water and salt together in a saucepan. Remove from heat and add Jello, ginger and water. Pour this liquid over ingredients in the pan and stir gently to separate cheese. Chill in refrigerator until firm. Cut in squares and serve on lettuce garnished with mayonnaise and parsley. Serves 10.

U. S. 101, 2 miles south of Quilcene, Washington

PAINTING BY PETE LONG

Mary's Italian Dinners A 50-YEAR-OLD

Colonial homestead houses this spacious Italian restaurant. Mary Palmerio, its owner and manager, has been in the food business for nearly 30 years.

Dinner until midnight daily.

PIZZA

Make enough bread dough for one average loaf of bread and let rise 2 times. Arrange a thin layer of dough on a metal cookie sheet which has an edge all around. Over the top spread 2 cups of tomatoes seasoned with salt and pepper. Italian sausage and anchovies may be added if desired. Sprinkle sparingly with salad oil or olive oil. Bake in preheated 350° oven for 20 minutes or until brown. Before removing from oven spread slices of provoloni or mozzarelli cheese over top and keep in oven until it begins to melt. Remove from oven, slice in individual pieces and serve hot. This recipe will make about 6 servings.

East 4235 Hartson Avenue, Spokane, Washington

Moscow Restaurant

NICHOLAS GORN, an ex-officer in the Tsar's army, and his wife Marie Gorn own and manage this authentic and colorful Russian restaurant.

Dinner, late supper, 5:00 p.m. to 1:00 a.m., except Sunday.

BORSCH

1 onion
2 carrots
1 stalk celery
½ pound cabbage
 Salt and pepper
1 teaspoon butter
½ cup tomato purée
5 cups beef stock
1 beet, boiled
 Sour cream

Shred onion, carrots, celery and cabbage. Season and fry lightly in butter; then add tomato purée. Pour in a little stock, simmer gently until vegetables are tender. Add finely shredded beet and remaining stock. Let soup boil once more. Serve hot or cold, topped with sour cream. This soup may be served as an appetizer. It also makes an excellent main dish for lunch.

5 WEST
192

763 Lakeview Boulevard, Seattle, Washington

The Dorchester House   THE DINING ROOMS

here overlook the Pacific Ocean. Overnight accommodations.

Breakfast, lunch, dinner daily.

CRAB LOUIE

Line a plate or platter with lettuce leaves. Fill in center with shredded lettuce. Add desired number of portions of crab meat. Top with Louie Dressing, sprinkle with chopped eggs, a ripe olive, crab legs, green pepper strips, tomato slices and a lemon wedge.

LOUIE DRESSING

To a quart of salad dressing add 1 cup chili sauce; ½ cup each, chopped egg, chopped celery, and a ½ cup chopped ripe olives. Mix and chill.

CLAM CHOWDER

Sauté 1 cup diced onion and 1 cup diced celery in a little butter. Boil 1 cup diced potatoes. Combine sautéed onions and celery with boiled potatoes and add to vegetables 1 cup chopped clams, 1 No. 2 can tomatoes and 3 cups chicken or beef broth. Season with salt and pepper. Bring to a boil, not too hard, and thicken slightly with a butter roux. Let simmer 5 minutes. Serves 8.

U. S. 101, Oceanlake, Oregon

Berg's Chalet THIS "COUNTRY spot in the city" is housed in a mansion that was once the home of Joseph Teal, a Columbia River steamship man. The house is still furnished in the original Honduras mahogany, and the wall coverings are 20-karat gold leaf and silk damask.

Lunch, noon to 2:00 p.m.; dinner, 5:00 p.m. to midnight. Reservations advisable.

SPECIAL PRIME RIBS BARBECUED IN SALT JACKET

10 pounds prime rib roast
12 cups flour
12 cups rock salt
    Pepper
    Garlic, if desired

Mix flour and salt together thoroughly. Add water to this mixture until it makes a firm dough. Rub beef with pepper and garlic. Roll dough about 1½ inches thick and mold over roast. Place in 350° oven 3½ hours for medium rare; about 4½ hours for well done. Break jacket with hammer and remove before serving roast.

5

WEST
194

741 S.W. St. Claire, Portland, Oregon

Pine Tavern MAREN GRIBSKEV is the owner and manager of this establishment, which began as a small lunch counter. It overlooks Mirror Pond and has a lovely garden reaching to the river's edge.

Breakfast, lunch, dinner, 7:00 a.m. to 9:00 p.m. Closed Sunday and holidays.

WILD RICE DRESSING

1½ cups wild rice
1 large onion, well minced
1 cup bacon drippings or butter
1½ loaves stale cracked wheat bread
1 cup cooked celery, chopped
2 teaspoons parsley, chopped
1 level teaspoon curry powder (optional)
Sage, if desired

Salt and pepper to taste
2 eggs, well beaten

Boil rice about 20 minutes in 3 quarts of water, drain well and cool. Fry onion in fat until clear. Crumb bread finely. Mix all ingredients, folding in beaten eggs last and toss dressing lightly. This recipe enough to stuff a 12 to 15 pound turkey. Delicious also with any other type of fowl or with veal and pork.

Foot of Oregon Avenue in downtown Bend, Oregon

The Round House

THE GLASS walls of this dining room, which is located at the southern end of the Golden Gate Bridge, afford patrons a view of the Bay area.

Breakfast, lunch, dinner daily.

PAN-FRIED CHICKEN

Chicken, cut up and rolled in seasoned flour
Frying fat
1 tablespoon water per pound chicken

Heat ½-to 1-inch layer of fat in a large skillet until a drop of water sizzles on it (about 350°). Place floured chicken in skillet. Start browning the meaty pieces first, skin side down, slipping less meaty pieces in between as chicken browns. Do not crowd. Use tongs or spoons for turning to avoid piercing through coating and skin. When chicken is uniformly brown, 15 to 20 minutes, reduce heat, add water, cover tightly and cook slowly until tender, 20 to 40 minutes, depending on size and thickness of pieces. Turn once or twice to assure even cooking. Uncover last 5 to 10 minutes to recrisp skin.

5

Golden Gate Bridge, San Francisco, California

PAINTING BY PARKER EDWARDS

Tarantino's Restaurant HERE IS an eating
place set amidst the famous Fishermen's Wharf.

Lunch, dinner, 11:00 a.m. to midnight daily.

HALIBUT FLORENTINE

   2 pounds halibut steak or filet

   ½ cup white wine

   Juice of 3 lemons

   1 cup heavy cream sauce

   8 ounces spinach, cooked and
      chopped

   3 green onions, finely chopped

   Salt and pepper to taste

   3 egg yolks

   ½ cup grated Italian cheese

Place halibut in shallow saucepan. Cover with water; add wine and lemon juice. Cover and boil 5 to 10 minutes or until liquid is reduced to one third. Remove halibut; place in baking dish. Place cream sauce in second saucepan, and add broth from halibut, spinach, onions, salt, and pepper. Mix and bring to a boil. Then remove from fire and stir in egg yolks. This gives you a Florentine sauce. Pour this sauce over halibut and sprinkle with grated cheese. Bake at 400° until golden brown. Serve hot from baking dish. Four portions.

206 Jefferson Street, Fishermen's Wharf, San Francisco, California   **WEST 5**

197

India House BRITISH-BORN David Brown has made this restaurant famous. The candle-lit dining room is hung with rare rice-paper water colors of Bengal tigers, and meals are served by Sikhs and Hindus in native costume.

Dinner, except Sunday. Reservations advisable.

JAWAHARLAL PANDIT'S LAMB CURRY

1 pound lamb
2 to 3 small onions
2 cloves garlic
3 tablespoons oil
1 tablespoon curry powder
¼ teaspoon cayenne pepper
1 teaspoon sugar
2 teaspoons grated coconut
2 cups stock

Slice onions, chop garlic and fry to light brown in oil. Add curry powder, pepper, sugar and coconut. Season to taste with salt. When well mixed, add the stock and simmer for 20 minutes, stirring occasionally. Add meat (after cutting in 1-inch cubes) and simmer for 1 hour, or until meat is tender. Serve very hot with rice and chutney.

5 **WEST**
198

629 Washington Street, San Francisco, California

PAINTING BY PARKER EDWARDS

Omar Khayyam's THE COMBINATION of superlative Armenian food and the colorful personality of owner George Mardikian have combined to make this restaurant one of the most famous in San Francisco.

Dinner, 4:00 p.m. to midnight daily.

KOUZOU KZARTMA

- 4 lamb shanks
- 2 cups water
- 2 tomatoes, quartered
- 2 teaspoons salt
- 1 teaspoon paprika
- 4 large pieces potato

Wash lamb and soak in water for 15 minutes. Cook for ½ hour at 375° in open roasting pan with tomatoes, salt, paprika and water. Turn meat over and cook another ½ hour. Add potatoes and roast 30 minutes more, then turn the meat and potatoes and roast another ½ hour. Serve with its own juice. This makes a complete meal for 4.

196 O'Farrell Street, San Francisco, California

Spenger's   THE PRESENT owner's father started this thriving business over 75 years ago. Today the concern's fishing boats daily bring in fresh seafood, which you may buy in the market or eat in the nautical dining room.

Lunch, dinner until 1:00 a.m. Closed Thanksgiving Day and Christmas Day.

FRANK SPENGER'S DELIGHT

6 slices filet of smelt, sole or any
    thin fish
  Flour
  Salt and pepper to taste
3 tablespoons olive oil
3 tablespoons butter
  Juice of 1 lemon
  Parsley

Dredge fish in mixture of flour, salt and pepper. Fry slowly in mixture of olive oil and butter until golden brown. Remove fish from frying pan to platter. Squeeze lemon juice into the drippings, stir and pour over fish. Serve piping hot. Garnish with chopped parsley.

5

WEST   *1919 Fourth Street, near University Avenue, Berkeley, California*
200

PAINTING BY PARKER EDWARDS

Yamato Sukiyaki House

In all but one large public room, meals are served Japanese-style. Shoes are removed and diners eat seated on straw mats.

Lunch, noon to 2:00 p.m.; dinner, 5:00 p.m. to 10:00 p.m. weekdays; Sunday dinner, 3:00 p.m. to 10:00 p.m. Closed Monday. Reservations advisable.

BEEF TERIYAKI

6 to 8 ounces steak, or other tender meat

1 ounce beef stock

½ teaspoon sugar

1 ounce soy sauce

1 jigger cooking wine (sherry or sake)

Dash fresh grated ginger

Pan-broil steak and slice into thin strips. Mix other ingredients with juice from pan-broiled meat, heat and pour over sliced steak. Or charcoal-broil steak and slice into bite-size chunks ready for serving. Add sauce over meat. Sauce may be thickened with cornstarch if desired. This recipe for 1 serving.

717 California Street, San Francisco, California

Frank Torres Beach Hotel

THE large windows in this establishment's dining room look out on golden sands, the Pacific Ocean, and rolling hills. Overnight accommodations. Reservations advisable.

Open 11:00 a.m. to 2:00 a.m., except Monday.

DINNER FOR FOUR

16 lamb kidneys or 2 beef kidneys, sliced
4 tablespoons vegetable oil
1 onion, chopped
½ pound mushrooms, sliced
2 cloves garlic, chopped
Salt and pepper, to taste
1 teaspoon parsley, chopped
4 tablespoons red wine
Rice or potatoes

Heat oil in skillet. Add kidneys and sauté quickly. Then add onion, mushrooms, garlic and seasoning. Cook over hot fire for 15 minutes. Add parsley and wine. Serve at once with rice or potatoes.

5 WEST
202

State Highway 1, Montara, California

PAINTING BY PARKER EDWARDS

Skipper Kent's   THIS South Seas dining room has doors flanked by Easter Island images.

Dinner, 6:00 p.m. to 11:30 p.m. weekdays; Sunday, 5:00 p.m. to 10:30 p.m. Reservations advisable.

SKIPPER'S CELESTIAL CHICKEN

For this recipe you will need the breast of a 4-pound roaster, ½ teaspoon red wine, ½ teaspoon soy sauce, 1 well-beaten egg, a pinch of Ac'cent, salt and pepper, flour (water chestnut, if possible), and fat for frying.

Skin and bone chicken and cut into large strips ¼ inch thick. Mix wine, soy, egg, Ac'cent and seasonings; sprinkle over chicken pieces with a spoon. Roll chicken in flour and pat in well. Fry in 350° fat for 5 to 6 minutes.

Drain on paper, cut chicken in 1-inch squares. Serve with cream sauce.

CREAM SAUCE

In a separate pan melt 2 tablespoons butter and blend in 1 heaping tablespoon flour until smooth. Slowly add 1 cup cream; salt and pepper to taste. Stir and cook until smooth. Add 4 ounces drained button mushrooms and heat through. Pour over chicken. Sprinkle with browned sesame seeds. Serves 4.

Rainbow Tavern THIS resort in the high Sierras, just 86 miles east of Sacramento, is open the year round. In the summer you may swim, hunt, and fish; in the winter, ski and skate. Overnight accommodations and vacation facilities.

Breakfast, lunch, dinner, 8:00 a.m. to 9:00 p.m. daily.

SWISS STEAK

2 pounds round or chuck steak
½ cup flour
2 teaspoons salt
½ teaspoon pepper
3 tablespoons fat
2 small onions
2 cups canned tomatoes
2 large carrots, diced
3 stalks celery, diced
1 small can mushrooms, diced
1 quart beef stock

Cut steak slices 1 to 2 inches thick. Mix flour, salt and pepper; pound into steak thoroughly. Brown meat and onions in hot fat before adding tomatoes, carrots, celery, mushrooms and beef stock. Bake in moderate oven (350° to 375°) for about 2 hours or until tender.

5

On U. S. 40, Soda Springs, California

Paso Robles Inn THIS inn is conveniently located midway between Los Angeles and San Francisco. Overnight accommodations. Reservations advisable.

Breakfast, lunch, dinner, 7:00 a.m. to 11:00 p.m.

BAKED PORK CHOP, ARABIAN STYLE

4 thick loin pork chops
Salt and pepper, to taste
1 medium size tomato, sliced
1 cup wild rice, cooked
1 medium onion, sliced
1 medium green pepper
4 slices Cheddar cheese
2 tablespoons fat

Season chops, then put a slice of tomato on each one, followed by a layer of wild rice (ordinary rice may be substituted), sliced onion and green pepper. Bake in 300° to 325° oven for 2 hours. Then top each chop with a slice of cheese and fat; leave in oven until cheese melts and runs over the sides. Serves 4.

1101 Spring Street (U.S. 101), Paso Robles, California

Babbling Brook THIS restaurant is named for the stream that winds through its garden dining room.

Lunch, dinner, except Sunday. Closed during December and January.

CHICKEN AND DUMPLINGS

Take 1 fat hen and cook whole or disjointed in 1½ quarts of water seasoned with salt. Cook for about 3 hours. When tender lift out of broth and cool. Pick meat from bones and cut in small pieces. Thicken broth with 7 tablespoons flour and ¾ cup water. Mix smooth with egg beater. Season to taste with salt and pepper. Add a few drops of yellow food coloring. Strain over chicken. Reserve 4 cups of gravy in a flat stew pan for dumplings.

DUMPLINGS

    1 egg
    ⅔ cup milk
    1 tablespoon oil or melted
      shortening
  1½ cups flour
    ⅔ teaspoon salt
    4 level teaspoons baking powder

Sift dry ingredients into liquid and stir briskly until blended. Drop dumpling batter by teaspoonfuls into boiling gravy. Cover and cook gently for 8 to 10 minutes or until done.

5

Off State Highway 1, 1025 Laurel Street, Santa Cruz, California

Apple Valley Inn

BUILT around a swimming pool, this year-round resort nestles in a desert basin, surrounded by the snow-capped peaks of the San Bernardino and Sierra Madre mountains. Overnight accommodations and vacation facilities.

Breakfast, lunch, dinner, 8:00 a.m. to 11:00 p.m. daily.

ANCIENT BARBECUE SAUCE

1 pound tallow
1 tablespoon sage
1 tablespoon thyme
1 tablespoon rosemary
1 pint olive oil
2 pints catsup
8 cloves garlic, crushed
1 pint steak sauce

Cook tallow for 20 minutes before adding spices and remaining ingredients. A really old recipe handed down for many generations, this sauce is excellent with spareribs, lamb, or beef. This sauce is featured weekly here at the famous outdoor steak fry.

On State Highway 18, Apple Valley, California

WEST 5

Santa Maria Inn

FOR over 35 years this inn, which is at the halfway point between Los Angeles and San Francisco, has been a favorite with travelers. Overnight accommodations. Reservations advisable.

Breakfast, lunch, dinner daily.

FIG PUDDING

7 eggs, separated
½ pound sugar
¾ pound white bread crumbs
½ pound preserved figs
½ pound butter, melted
½ teaspoon allspice
    Vanilla and brandy to taste

Beat egg yolks and add sugar. Add beaten egg whites. Beat well. Add bread crumbs, figs, butter, allspice, vanilla and brandy to taste. Pour into two-quart mold, and steam 4 to 5 hours. Use a hard sauce for topping. Serves 12.

5

WEST

U. S. 101, Santa Maria, California

PAINTING BY YALE GRACEY

Farmer John's THIS typical Early California ranch-type restaurant specializes in fried chicken, steaks, and prime ribs. On sunny days guests enjoy their meals on the outdoor dining patio. Overnight accommodations.

Lunch, dinner, except Monday.

FRIED CHICKEN

The chef here serves 1 pound of chicken to a portion. An eviscerated chicken is unjointed and marinated for 15 minutes in whole milk seasoned with salt and pepper. Then the chicken pieces are dipped in flour and fried in enough fat to cover the chicken. Fry until two-thirds done; finish cooking in oven. Try finishing the meal with Farmer John's famous dessert—a chocolate nut sundae, served in a small flower pot, with a real flower stuck in it.

630 N. Sepulveda Boulevard, West Los Angeles, California

Brookdale Lodge THOUSANDS of visitors, from school children to presidents, have stopped to admire this amazing dining room, which is divided by a natural mountain stream, flanked by ferns and trees. Overnight accommodations and vacation facilities. Reservations necessary.

Breakfast, lunch, dinner daily.

BROOKDALE LODGE DRESSING

¼ pound Gorgonzola cheese, crumbled
2 cloves garlic, chopped or mashed
¼ teaspoon salt
¼ teaspoon pepper, freshly ground
2 tablespoons wine vinegar
1 tablespoon Worcestershire sauce
½ cup olive oil

Combine all ingredients and let stand in a warm place until flavor works through, stirring occasionally. (If Gorgonzola cheese is not available, try blue cheese or Roquefort.)

On State Highway 9, Brookdale, California

Rand's Round-up   RAY RAND is the owner and manager of this spot, famous for its chuck-wagon dinners.

Lunch, dinner, after-theater supper daily. Sunday morning brunch.

CHEESE BLINTZES

    2 eggs
    2 cups water
    ⅛ teaspoon vanilla
    2 cups flour
    ⅛ teaspoon nutmeg
    4 tablespoons sugar
    ¾ teaspoon baking powder
    ⅛ teaspoon salt

Beat eggs and add water and vanilla. Blend dry ingredients and combine with egg mixture with a few strokes. Heat a 5-inch skillet and grease with a few drops of oil. Add small amount of batter and tip skillet to spread batter over bottom. Brown on one side only and turn out on a plate brown-side up. Fry all the blintzes.

FILLING

Combine 6 ounces dry cottage cheese and 6 ounces cream cheese and place a spoonful of this mixture on each blintz. Fold blintz edges toward middle so they lap over filling. Return blintzes to skillet and sauté in butter on both sides until lightly browned. Serve with powdered sugar and sour cream. Makes about 15 blintzes.

7580 Sunset Boulevard, Hollywood, California

Pierpont Inn

THIS eating place is situated on a bluff overlooking the Pacific Ocean and the Channel Islands. Overnight accommodations and vacation facilities.

Breakfast, lunch, dinner daily.

CURRIED SHRIMP IN CASSEROLE

2½ pounds fresh, cleaned shrimp
1 onion, chopped
2 bay leaves
2 tablespoons salt
1 teaspoon pepper
¼ pound butter
1 cup flour
3 tablespoons curry powder
2 cups cooked rice

Cook shrimp in water with bay leaves, onion, half of salt and pepper. Save 1 quart broth. Blend flour and butter; make sauce, using broth. Add curry and remaining salt and pepper. Add most of shrimp. Line 8 individual casseroles with remaining shrimp and top with curried shrimp. Serve piping hot.

Four blocks south of U. S. 101, Ventura, California

Chinese Village Cafe GEORGE JOE is the owner and manager of this famous Cantonese restaurant.

Open 4:00 p.m. to 4:00 a.m. daily. Reservations necessary.

EGG ROLL

3 eggs
1 quart cooking oil
1 cup fresh bean sprouts
½ cup celery, finely diced
½ cup pork strips, finely sliced
½ teaspoon salt
¼ teaspoon pepper

Beat 2 eggs until well blended. Pour half of eggs into a heavy 8-inch frying pan that has been lightly greased and heated. Cook quickly on one side. Turn over with a wide spatula so the egg remains as a large thin pancake. Cook until done. Prepare remaining egg the same way. Combine other ingredients (except oil and third egg); divide them between the 2 egg rolls. Fold lower third of egg roll over filling. Turn the ends in about ½ inch to seal. Brush the top third of egg roll with slightly beaten egg to seal and fold this over the rolled mixture. Place the rolls in a basket and steam 20 minutes. Then brown in 2 inches of 350° oil. Brown rolls about 3 to 5 minutes on each side. Serve hot with mustard and soy sauce. Serves 4.

Kover's Bull Pen THE OWNERS of this modern restaurant, Ruth and Edward Kover, are a former dance team, who have turned their talents to food, with the result that their names are now synonymous with outstanding cookery.

Open 24 hours daily.

COLESLAW—OREGON STYLE

2 pounds cabbage, shredded
1 carrot, shredded
1 bunch parsley, chopped
1 bunch green onions, chopped
1 cup granulated sugar
¾ cup salad oil

1 cup vinegar
2 teaspoons salt
1 teaspoon pure black pepper

Toss together well and serve immediately, while greens are fresh and crisp.

5
WEST
214

14649 Ventura Boulevard, Sherman Oaks (Los Angeles), California

The Cock 'n Bull
OLD prints, pewter, brass, and copper add to the English atmosphere, which has been created by owner John Morgan.

Lunch, dinner, snacks, noon to 2:00 a.m. Hunt breakfast Sunday, 10:00 a.m. to 2:30 p.m. Reservations necessary for dinner.

CORNISH PASTY

    Pie dough to cover sides of 10 x 18 inch pan, 3 inches deep, and for top crust
2 pounds diced beef
1 large onion, sliced very thin
2 large potatoes, diced
    Salt and white pepper, to taste
½ cup beef stock or finely ground suet

Line pan with pie dough. Add a layer of diced beef, a layer of onion, and then potatoes and seasonings. Repeat this process until pan is reasonably full. Add beef stock or suet. Cover top with crust. Bake about 1½ hours in a 350° oven. This recipe will serve 12.

MUSTARD SAUCE

Mix together 2 tablespoons mustard, ½ tablespoon sugar, pinch of salt, 1 tablespoon melted butter, and ½ cup vinegar. Serve with hot or cold lamb.

The Victor Hugo Inn

SET in the midst of three elegant formal gardens on a bluff overlooking the wave-swept shores of Laguna Bay, this restaurant is almost as famous for its setting as for its cuisine.

Lunch, dinner, except Monday. Closed first two weeks in December.

CRÈME VICHYSSOISE

4 leeks
1 medium onion
2 ounces sweet butter
4 medium-sized Idaho potatoes
1 quart chicken broth
4 cups 18% cream
Salt and pepper
1 cup sour cream
Chopped chives

Slice the white part of the leeks and finely chop onion; then cook together in butter. Then add quartered potatoes and chicken broth. Boil fast for 30 minutes. Mash, then strain through fine cheese cloth and add 18% cream. Season to taste and bring to boil. Cool and strain again through fine muslin cloth and add sour cream and chill. Serve this soup ice cold, topped with chives.

5

WEST
216

361 Cliff Drive, Laguna Beach, California

Christian's Hut NAMED for Fletcher Christian of "Mutiny on the Bounty" fame, this eating place commands a magnificent view of Balboa Bay.

Dinner. Closed Monday from October 1 to March 1. Reservations necessary during summer.

PITCAIRN SALAD DRESSING

1 quart mayonnaise
½ pound Roquefort cheese
1 tablespoon Worcestershire
    sauce
1 cup vinegar
4 tablespoons chopped chives
½ cup sugar

Mix well and pour over your favorite salad. Remainder can be stored in a tightly lidded jar in the refrigerator. At Christian's it is popular with a variety of salads, so try it on your favorite soon.

325 Edgewater, Balboa, California

The Golden Stallion   FRANK GEE is the owner and manager of this fine Chinese restaurant, located in Western movie-set territory, in the California desert. Overnight accommodations and vacation facilities.

Breakfast, lunch, dinner, except Monday.

CHINESE GREEN PEA CHOW YOKE

2 cups roast pork or beef, diced
2 medium-sized onions, chopped
2 tablespoons peanut oil
1 cup mushrooms
1 cup celery, chopped
1 cup water chestnuts
2½ cups bamboo shoots
2 cups green peas, rinsed with boiling water

Salt and pepper
1 tablespoon soy sauce

Sauté onions in peanut oil until they are golden brown. Mix diced meat and other ingredients together (except soy). Add to onions; simmer covered 15 minutes. Remove cover and cook 10 minutes, over medium fire. Add soy sauce. Stir occasionally. Serves 6.

5

WEST   *Take 29 Palms Road to Yucca, turn off to Pioneertown, California*

PAINTING BY JON CORNIN

Danville Hotel Restaurant THIS hostelry, built in 1892, was a stagecoach stop for many years.

Dinner weekdays; Sunday dinner, 2:00 to 10:00 p.m. Closed Tuesday. Reservations advisable week ends.

FRIED CAMEMBERT CHEESE

Cut Camembert cheese in desired portions, after removing rind. Dip in beaten eggs and fresh bread crumbs. Harden in refrigerator. Before serving fry very quickly in hot, deep grease. Currant jelly or Bar-le-Duc and melba toast may be served with it.

OYSTER BROCHETTE MONTEBELLO

Wrap 6 raw oysters and 6 fresh mushroom heads separately in bacon and alternate on skewers. Dip in mixture of 1 cup oil, 1 teaspoon salt, 1 teaspoon English mustard and pinch of pepper. Roll in crumbs and fry in butter 25 minutes. Serve with lemon butter.

On State Highway 21, north of Oakland, Danville, California

Golden Nugget IF after a hard day's ride you've come upon a good eating place only to find it closed, you'll appreciate this establishment, which is open 24 hours a day. In keeping with the tradition of the town, the walls are lined with paintings of the gold-rush days.

Open 24 hours daily.

BAKED PORK CHAMPVALLON

8 ½-inch thick pork chops
2 pounds potatoes, sliced
½ pound onions, sliced thin
  Salt and white pepper
  Chicken or beef broth

Dip pork chops in flour and sauté until brown. Mix potatoes and onion slices together. Place half on the bottom of a baking pan, lay pork chops over them and then another layer of potatoes and onions. Season with salt and white pepper. Add broth to level with the ingredients. Cover pan and bake 45 minutes at 350°.

Second and Fremont Streets, Las Vegas, Nevada

Swiss Village Restaurant MARION and Walter Wolfinger own and manage this fine restaurant, which serves American and Continental foods.

Breakfast, lunch, dinner, 7:00 a.m. to 10:00 p.m.

SWISS VEAL SAUTÉ

2 pounds top round leg of veal
1 medium onion, chopped fine
4 ounces butter
½ pound fresh mushrooms
½ pint white wine
1 quart brown gravy
1 teaspoon salt
Dash of pepper
Egg noodles
Nutmeg

Cut ¼-inch thick veal into 1-inch cubes and sauté with chopped onion and butter in a skillet until light golden brown. Add fresh mushrooms and white wine. Simmer 3 to 4 minutes. Then add gravy and simmer 5 minutes longer. Season. Serve with hot, buttered egg noodles, sprinkled lightly with nutmeg. Serves 6.

116 North Fifth Street, Las Vegas, Nevada

Shore Lodge ON Payette Lake in the mountains, this friendly resort is 108 miles north of Boise, Idaho. To eliminate a constant complaint, each room has a lake view. Overnight accommodations and vacation facilities.

Breakfast, lunch, dinner, 7:00 a.m. to 10:00 p.m. daily.

FRIED CORN MEAL MUSH

4 cups boiling water
1½ teaspoons salt
1½ cups corn meal
1 cup chopped ham or bacon
Parsley, to taste
1 egg
Cracker crumbs and flour
Bacon slices, cooked
Molasses or maple syrup

Add salt and corn meal to boiling water and cook well. Then add ham and parsley. Pour into a well-greased loaf pan and cool. Cut into slices ½ inch thick and roll in mixture of egg, cracker crumbs and flour. Fry to a golden brown. Strip with bacon slices and top with molasses or maple syrup. Makes 6 servings.

State Highway 15, McCall, Idaho

Sun Valley   WORLD famous for skiing, this mountain resort appeals no less to equestrians. Reservations suggested.

Breakfast, lunch, dinner. Closed October 15 to December 18.

APPLE PANCAKES

Whip 4 eggs; then add 1 pint coffee cream, ½ grated lemon rind, ¼ grated orange rind, dash of vanilla, 4 tablespoons sugar, ¼ tablespoon salt, and pinch of nutmeg. Mix and add 1¾ cups flour. Peel and slice 3 medium apples; sprinkle with cinnamon and sugar and fry lightly. Add 2 ounces whipped cream to batter just before frying. Heat an 8- or 10-inch skillet. Put in 6-ounce ladle of batter per pancake and cook slowly on one side; add apples, and then turn over and put in 325° oven for 5 minutes. Take out of oven and turn, sprinkle with cinnamon, sugar and return to oven for 1 to 2 minutes. Put on plate and serve with lemon wedge. Serves 8. (Do not use syrup as pancakes are very sweet.)

On U. S. 93, 1 mile northeast of Ketchum, Idaho

Wagon Wheel Lodge THIS lodge offers year-round vacationing in the heart of one of Colorado's finest recreation areas. Overnight accommodations.

Breakfast, lunch, dinner. Closed December 22 to February 1.

WAGON WHEEL HUB ROLLS

1 cake yeast
¼ cup warm water
½ cup condensed milk
1 cup water
1 teaspoon salt
¼ cup sugar
¼ cup shortening
2¼ cups flour

Soak yeast in warm water. Mix milk with 1 cup water and scald. Then add salt, sugar, shortening; cool to luke-warm. Then add half the flour. Mix well. Add soaked yeast mixture and balance of flour. Mix well and place in greased bowl until it rises. Grease hands and mold dough into pieces, a little larger than a walnut, drop in hot fat and fry until golden brown. Eat immediately with honey or jam. Dough will keep in the refrigerator for 3 days, wrapped in a towel or waxed paper.

5

WEST
224

Off State Highway 119 to Gold Hill Road, Boulder, Colorado

Corner Cupboard Inn

THIS delightful mountain resort is situated on the shores of Colorado's largest natural lake, on the western border of Rocky Mountain National Park. Overnight facilities.

Breakfast, lunch, dinner. Closed September 21 to June 12.

FUDGE CAKE

1 cup milk
3 squares chocolate
1 cup sugar
⅓ cup butter
2 eggs
1 teaspoon soda
1½ cups sifted flour
½ teaspoon baking powder
Pinch of salt
1 teaspoon vanilla

Warm ½ cup milk and cook chocolate in it; then let cool. Blend sugar with butter, beat in eggs and remaining ½ cup milk. Dissolve soda in a little hot water and beat in flour, baking powder, salt and vanilla. Then blend 3 mixtures together. Makes 2 9-inch or 3 small layers. Bake in 350° oven 20 minutes. Frost with fudge icing.

On State Highway 278, 1 mile from U. S. 34, Grand Lake, Colorado

PAINTING BY FRANCES LAKE MC KENNA

Brown Palace Hotel   THE PALACE ARMS is
the newest dining room in this famous Denver landmark. The
décor is developed around authentic copies of 22 flags, famous
in American history prior to 1830. Overnight accommodations
and vacation facilities.

Lunch, dinner daily. Reservations advisable.

FRENCH PANCAKES

6 ounces cream
1 cup flour
8 eggs
1 tablespoon sugar
Pinch of salt
Grated rind of 1 orange
3 tablespoons melted butter
5 cups creamed chicken
2 cups Hollandaise sauce

Whip the cream and then add the
flour. Beat eggs, sugar, salt, butter and
rind together. Add flour mixture slowly
to eggs. Batter should be thin. Cook in
a 6-inch pan that is hot and dry. This
recipe makes approximately 24 pancakes. Put creamed chicken on pancakes and roll them up. Top with Hollandaise and put in the oven to brown.
Serve immediately. Makes 8 servings.

5

WEST
226

17th and Tremont Streets, Denver, Colorado

Crystal River Lodge

ONCE a 2½-million-dollar private estate, this lodge, in the heart of the Rockies, is now a popular overnight stop and vacation spot. It is owned and managed by C. D. Cook.

Breakfast, lunch, dinner. Closed November 1 to May 15.

CHESTNUT DRESSING

- ⅓ cup pork sausage
- 1 cup ground chestnuts
- 3 cups bread crumbs
- 1 apple, cut in small pieces
- 1 tablespoon onion, chopped
- 1 tablespoon parsley, chopped
- Salt and pepper, to taste

Fry pork sausage, then mix all ingredients together. This recipe makes enough to stuff about a 10-pound turkey.

QUICKIE DESSERT

Into a sherbet dish break 2 graham crackers. Pour pineapple juice over them and top with a generous helping of whipped cream. Top with a cherry.

On State Highway 133, near Redstone, Colorado

Zietz Buckhorn Restaurant THE atmosphere of this interesting dining spot has remained practically unchanged since it was founded in 1873 by the late Henry Zietz, an old-time Indian scout and protégé of Buffalo Bill Cody. Henry Zietz, Jr., is the owner and manager.

Lunch, dinner, except Sunday. Reservations necessary.

ZIETZ FAMOUS BEAN SOUP

  2 quarts cooked navy beans
  2 cups cooked ham, diced
  1 small onion, minced
    Salt and pepper, to taste

Combine beans and liquid with ham and ham liquor. Add minced onion and simmer mixture for about 15 minutes. Season to taste. This recipe yields 6 to 8 portions. You can make a complete meal of this nourishing soup.

5

WEST
228

1000 Osage Street, Denver, Colorado

Holiday Inn VACATIONISTS who like their outdoor life accompanied by all the modern conveniences and good food thoroughly enjoy this vacation spot. Overnight accommodations are offered, too.

Breakfast, lunch, dinner. Closed May 20 to October 15.

SCRAPPLE, HOLIDAY INN STYLE

        3 pounds pork neck bones
        2 quarts boiling, salted water
    1½ cups corn meal
        2 cups cold water
    ½ teaspoon pepper
        Salt, to taste
    1 teaspoon thyme and sage, mixed

Simmer neck bones 2 hours in boiling, salted water, until meat can be easily removed from bones. Remove meat and bones and strain broth. Shred meat finely and add to strained stock. Mix corn meal and cold water. Stir into boiling stock and meat. Cook until thickened; add the seasonings. Pour thoroughly thickened scrapple into loaf cake pans which have been dipped in water. Chill. Then slice and fry like corn meal mush. Serve hot with butter and syrup.

On U. S. 24 (west of Colorado Springs), Hartsel, Colorado

PAINTING BY PAUL GALLAGHER

Toklat Wilderness Lodge   AT this lodge,
which is owned by Isabel and Stuart Mace, the flour for the
bread is stone-ground. Overnight, vacation facilities.

Breakfast, lunch, dinner.

HAM SNAILS

For this recipe you will need 1½
cups sifted bread flour, 1 tablespoon
baking powder, ½ teaspoon salt, 1
tablespoon sesame seed, 3 tablespoons
shortening, ½ cup milk, melted butter,
1½ cups ground ham.

Mix flour, baking powder and salt.
Add sesame seed. Then cut in shortening; moisten with milk. Roll dough into
½-inch thick rectangle. Brush with butter and spread ham evenly over the surface. Roll like a jelly roll. Cut into 1
inch slices. Bake on a cookie sheet 25
to 30 minutes at 400°. Serve with hot
basil tomato sauce.

SAUCE

Sauté 1 ground onion in 2 tablespoons butter. Combine 2 tablespoons
flour, 1 teaspoon sugar, 1 teaspoon salt
and ¼ teaspoon finely ground basil and
blend into onion mixture. To this add 1
cup canned tomatoes; cook till smooth.

Castle Creek Road, south of Aspen, Ashcroft, Colorado

The Village Inn   HOUSED in an interesting old stone church building, this restaurant specializes in Italian and American dishes and fine seafood.

Lunch, dinner, except Monday.

MUSHROOM SAUCE—VILLAGE INN

1 cup minced onion

¾ cup chopped green peppers

1 cup fresh sautéed mushrooms

2 cloves of garlic, crushed

1 teaspoon tomato paste

1 jigger Burgundy wine

1½ quarts brown gravy

Combine all of these ingredients and simmer for 1 hour.

At the Village Inn this sauce is a favorite. It is usually served over such dishes as chopped steak or roast beef.

Johnny Appleseed   RUTH AND GEORGE SNOW

own and manage this establishment, famous for its meats barbecued over apple wood and for its desserts.

Dinner, 5:00 p.m. to 10:00 p.m. weekdays; Sunday dinner, noon to 10:00 p.m.

APPLE CREAM PIE

CRUST

1⅛ cups sifted flour
½ teaspoon salt
⅜ cup shortening
⅛ cup cold milk

Sift flour and salt together. Cut in shortening until pieces are the size of peas. Add cold milk. Mix together and roll out for 9-inch pie crust. (This is a 1-crust pie.)

FILLING

5 apples, quartered
½ cup water
½ cup sugar
½ cup whipping cream
1 egg, beaten

Cook apples with sugar and water until tender. Remove apples; place carefully in crust. Beat egg and cream until light; then add apple juice. Pour over apples and bake in 350° oven for about 25 minutes until crust is done.

5

WEST
232

1114 South Nevada Avenue, Colorado Springs, Colorado

El Rancho Hotel and Courts ON the famous U. S. 66, this Western-style establishment welcomes guests from every part of the world. Overnight accommodations.

Breakfast, lunch, dinner, 6:00 a.m. to 10:00 p.m. daily.

SPANISH OMELET

4 thin slices bacon, minced
1 tomato, diced
1 onion, chopped
1 green pepper, chopped
5 mushrooms, chopped
6 eggs
3 tablespoons milk
½ teaspoon salt
⅛ teaspoon red pepper
1 tablespoon butter

Brown bacon, add tomato, onion, green pepper, mushrooms. Cook slowly 15 minutes, stirring occasionally. Beat eggs with milk, salt, red pepper. Melt butter in another pan and pour eggs in. Fry slowly until eggs are set. Pour part of sauce from first pan over eggs. Fold omelet and turn onto a hot platter. Cover with remaining sauce. Serves 6.

On U. S. 66, east of Gallup, New Mexico

WEST **5**

PAINTING BY ALLEN C. REED

Paint Pony Lodge

A BEAUTIFUL rustic retreat, this lodge is located high in the White Mountains. Overnight accommodations and vacation facilities. Experienced guides available. Reservations advisable.

Meals served to house guests only.

PAINT PONY CORNED BEEF

8- to 10-pound corned beef brisket
½ teaspoon each, oregano and
    rosemary
3 bay leaves
3 to 4 stalks parsley or celery tops
2 large garlic buds
1 tablespoon dill seed
2 medium-sized onions, quartered
1 teaspoon each, nutmeg,
    cinnamon and ground cloves

1 lemon, quartered
2 oranges, quartered
1 tablespoon Liquid Smoke
    (optional)
1 green pepper, quartered

Cover meat with hot water, add other ingredients and simmer gently for 5 to 6 hours. Or, better, simmer uncovered in a 250° oven 5 to 6 hours, turning meat once or twice during cooking.

On U. S. 60, northeast of Phoenix, Show Low, Arizona

PAINTING BY ALLEN C. REED

Frontier Inn Many east-west travelers go through Wickenburg especially to stop at Vic Comer's inn and see the barbecue ovens, where meat and poultry are smoked.

Open 11:00 a.m. to 9:00 p.m., except Tuesday and Christmas Day. Closed during July and August.

FRONTIER SALAD

6 slices bacon
1 clove garlic
2 cups peas, well drained
1 small onion, chopped fine
½ cup celery, sliced thin
½ cup sharp cheese, cut in small pieces
3 hard-boiled eggs, cut up fine
1 teaspoon Ac'cent
½ cup mayonnaise

Fry bacon, not too crisp, drain and cut in small pieces. Chill. Rub mixing bowl lightly with garlic. Mix vegetables, cheese, eggs, and bacon; top with Ac'cent. Let stand at room temperature for one hour. Mix with mayonnaise, just enough to bind together. Chill in refrigerator at least 1 hour. Serves 8.

466 East Center Street, east of Wickenburg, Arizona

Hotel Florence AT this perfect vacation spot, meals are served in the Chief Coffee Shop.

Breakfast, lunch, dinner daily.

BREAST OF CHICKEN DE LUXE

2 chicken breasts (3-pound chicken)
½ pint cream
½ teaspoon Angostura bitters
2 tablespoons flour
Paprika, salt and white pepper
4 ounces butter
½ pint milk
1 wine glass sherry wine
2 slices broiled ham
2 slices French toast
6 whole mushrooms, sautéed in butter

Place chicken breasts in a little cream with bitters added. Let stand for an hour. Then dredge in flour mixed with paprika; fry in butter until a golden brown. Make a roux of the remaining butter, flour, and seasonings. Scald rest of cream and milk; pour into roux, stirring constantly. Strain and put chicken in to simmer for 20 minutes. Before serving add wine to sauce. Place a slice of boiled ham on both pieces of toast. Top with chicken, mushrooms, and sauce. Serves 2.

5

WEST
236

111 North Higgins Avenue, Missoula, Montana

Rocky Mountain Cafe   THIS eating place is owned and managed by Gabriel Teddy Traparish.

Dinner, 5:00 p.m. to 1:00 a.m.

RAVIOLI

FILLING: Grind together 3 fried pork chops, 1 fried veal sirloin steak and ½ boiled chicken. To make paste, mix meat and fowl thoroughly with ½ pound spinach, chopped fine and fried in butter or olive oil; ½ bunch parsley; 2 eggs; 4 tablespoons grated Parmesan cheese; 2 cups bread crumbs soaked in broth, and seasoned to taste with all-spice, thyme, salt, pepper and a dash of garlic juice (optional).

PASTRY: Roll soft noodle dough very thin to form 2 sheets. Place dabs of fill-ing on one sheet 2 inches apart. Cover with second sheet and press down around filling. Cut around each mound with pastry wheel. Boil 15 to 20 min-utes in salted water, then drain thor-oughly.

SAUCE: Dice and sauté 2 stalks celery with 1 medium onion. Add 1 No. 2½ can of tomatoes and simmer for 20 min-utes. Add ½ can diluted tomato paste. Chop in parsley and garlic. Season with salt, pepper, allspice, thyme, nutmeg. Simmer for 1 hour. Serve over ravioli.

The Crossroads Inn   LOCATED at the junction of U. S. 10 and 12, east of Miles City, this inn is aptly named The Crossroads.

Dinner, 6:00 p.m. to 2:00 a.m. weekdays; Sunday dinner, 5:00 p.m. to 2:00 a.m. Reservations advised for Sunday Buffet.

SHRIMP-FRIED RICE

½ cup celery, chopped fine
¾ cup onion, chopped fine
1 cup green pepper, chopped fine
1 very small clove garlic, crushed
5 tablespoons bacon fat or oil
2 cups cooked shrimp, diced
½ cup mushrooms
4 cups cold, cooked rice
2 tablespoons pimento, chopped
4 tablespoons soy sauce

Simmer celery, onion, green pepper and garlic in fat for 5 minutes, in a heavy 10-inch frying pan, stirring occasionally. Add shrimp and mushrooms and cook another 3 minutes. Then stir in rice, pimentos, and soy sauce. Cook over moderate flame, stirring occasionally until mixture is hot. Serve immediately. Makes 6 portions.

5

WEST
238

U. S. 10 and 12, east of Miles City, Montana

Jack Moore's Open Range A CHARCOAL

broiler in the dining room is a feature of this restaurant, the oldest in town.

Lunch, dinner. Closed November 15 to May 15.

GUACAMOLE DRESSING

    1 medium avocado
    1 small onion
    2 teaspoons sugar
    1 tablespoon lemon juice
    1 teaspoon Worcestershire sauce
    Dash of Tabasco
    ⅛ teaspoon powdered garlic
    ⅛ teaspoon Ac'cent

    1 drop green food coloring
    1 cup pure mayonnaise

Grind the avocado and onion into a mixing bowl. Add sugar, lemon juice and seasonings to this mixture. Stir, blending thoroughly. Add the coloring and mayonnaise and stir until smooth. Serve on crisp lettuce or any green salad. This dressing is also delicious as a sauce for seafood cocktail.

On U. S. 187 and 89, Jackson, Wyoming

The Chuck Wagon   THIS establishment is patterned after a chuck wagon on an old-time cattle roundup. Food is cooked outdoors over wood fires and gains a delicious flavor from the smoke.

Open 10:30 a.m. to 9:00 p.m. Open June 2 to Labor Day.

ROUND-UP STEW

2½ pounds stew meat, diced
½ cup suet, diced
½ teaspoon pepper
4 teaspoons salt
1 teaspoon paprika
8 carrots, chopped
3 medium onions
6 spuds, cut small
4 stalks celery, chopped
¼ small cabbage

Braise meat and suet in Dutch oven, add seasonings and water to cover. Cook 2 hours, add carrots, cook 15 minutes. Then add remaining vegetables, except cabbage, which is added when other vegetables are cooked. Leave 10 minutes and serve. Water will evaporate so check while cooking.

5

WEST
240

On U. S. 26, 187, and 89, at Moose, Wyoming

PAINTING BY JOHN ENGELBART

Old Faithful Inn

THOUSANDS of tourists stop annually at this summer hotel in the western section of Yellowstone National Park. It is about 153 miles north of Idaho Falls, Idaho, and as the name implies is near the Park's most popular attraction, Old Faithful Geyser.

Breakfast, lunch, dinner. Closed September 15 to June 18. Reservations necessary.

POTATO PANCAKES

3 cups raw potatoes, finely grated
1 small onion, grated
1 tablespoon parsley, chopped
1 teaspoon salt
⅛ teaspoon pepper
1 egg
5 tablespoons flour
½ teaspoon baking powder

Combine potatoes and onion and then stir in other ingredients in the order listed. Bake on a medium-hot grill. This recipe will make about 16 medium pancakes.

Old Faithful, Yellowstone National Park, Wyoming

Index of Restaurants in This Book

RESTAURANTS ARE LISTED IN REGULAR LIGHT-FACE TYPE, STATES IN **BOLDFACE** (Canadian provinces are listed in *italics* under Canada) AND CITIES IN *italics*.

Index of Recipes in This Book

Restaurants Listed in Previous Ford Treasury

ALABAMA: Blue Moon Inn, 1524 Goode St., Montgomery; **Purefoy Hotel,** U.S. 241, Talladega

ARIZONA: El Merendero, 2702 N. Campbell, Tucson; **El Tovar Hotel,** State Highway 64, Grand Canyon

ARKANSAS: Crescent Hotel, Eureka Springs; **Hotel Sam Peck,** Capitol and Gaines Sts., Little Rock

CALIFORNIA: Andersen's, U.S. 101, Buellton; **Brown Derby,** 1628 North Vine St., Hollywood; **Café Caliente,** 20 Olvera St., Los Angeles; **Cathay House,** 718 California St., San Francisco; **Cliff House,** Great Highway at Seal Rocks, San Francisco; **Cold Spring Tavern,** State Highway 150, Santa Barbara; **Don the Beachcomber,** 1727 N. McCadden Place, Hollywood; **Fishermen's Grotto,** Number 9 Fishermen's Wharf, San Francisco; **Harbor Restaurant,** End of the Pier, Santa Barbara; **Holiday House,** 1270 Prospect St., La Jolla; **Hotel Bel-Air,** 701 Stone Canyon Road, Los Angeles; **Irons' Cottage by the Sea,** 501 Esplanade, Redondo Beach; **La Avenida Café,** 1301 Orange Ave., Coronado; **Locatelli's Inn,** Big Basin Highway, Boulder Creek; **L'Omelette French Restaurant,** 4170 El Camino Real, Palo Alto; **Mattei's Tavern,** Los Olivos; **Nut Tree,** U.S. 40, Vacaville; **Padua Hills Restaurant,** Padua Hills, Claremont; **Palace Hotel,** Market and New Montgomery Sts., San Francisco; **Tail o' the Cock,** 477 South La Cienega, Los Angeles; **Town House,** Commonwealth and Wilshire Blvd., Los Angeles; **Trader Vic's,** 6500 San Pablo Ave., Oakland; **Trinity Alps Resort,** Trinity Alps

COLORADO: Baldpate Inn, State Highway 7, Estes Park; **Country Kitchen,** U.S. 85 and 87, Littleton; **Riverside Lodge and Ranch,** State Highway 7, Lyons; **Stagecoach Inn,** 100 Manitou Ave., Manitou Springs; **Tepees,** U.S. 40, Golden

CONNECTICUT: Country Squire Inn, State Highway 80, Killingworth; **Dorlon's Shore House,** Dorlon's Point, Norwalk; **Fox Hill,** U.S. 7, Ridgefield; **Old Riverton Inn,** State Highway 20, Riverton; **Red Barn,** Merritt Parkway (Exit 41), Westport; **Skipper's Dock,** Noank; **Stonehenge,** U.S. 7, Ridgefield; **Westleigh Inn,** U.S. 25, Litchfield

DELAWARE: Winkler's, 1419 French St., Wilmington

DISTRICT OF COLUMBIA: Iron Gate Inn, 1734 N St., NW, Washington; **O'Donnell's Sea Grill,** 1221 E St., NW, Washington

FLORIDA: Châlet Suzanne, U.S. 27, Lake Wales; **Columbia Restaurant,** 22nd and 7th Ave., Tampa; **Dolphin Tavern,** State Highway A1A, Marineland; **Duck Inn,** 3974 Orange Blossom Trail, Orlando; **Garden,** 2235 Southwest Eighth St., Miami; **Lighthouse,** Baker's Haulover, Route A1A, Miami Beach; **Loffler Brothers' Oyster House,** 280 Alhambra Circle, Coral Gables

GEORGIA: Georgian Tea Room, 23 Abercorn St., Savannah

HAWAII: Broiler, 2416 Kalakaua Ave., Honolulu; **Don the Beachcomber,** Waikiki Beach, Honolulu; **Willows,** 901 Hausten St., Honolulu

IDAHO: Challenger Inn, Sun Valley

ILLINOIS: Boston Oyster House (Morrison Hotel), Chicago; **Brick House,** 402 Lincolnway West, Morrison; **Ernest Rickett's,** 103 East Chicago Ave., Chicago; **Fanny's,** 1601 Simpson St., Evanston; **Klas' Restaurant,** 5734 West Cermak Road, Cicero; **Pantry,** 718 Garden St., Park Ridge; **Pump Room** (Hotel Ambassador East), Chicago; **Urbana-Lincoln Hotel,** 209 South Broadway, Urbana; **Well-of-the-Sea** (Hotel Sherman), Chicago

INDIANA: Hawthorne Room, North Meridian at 16th St., Indianapolis; **Kopper Kettle,** U.S. 52, Morristown; **Nashville House,** Main and Van Buren Sts., Nashville

KENTUCKY: Beaumont Inn, State Highway 35, Harrodsburg; **Boone Tavern,** Berea College Campus, Berea; **Oelsner's Colonial Tavern,** U.S. 25 and 42, Covington; **Old House Restaurant,** 432 South Fifth St., Louisville; **Old Talbott Tavern,** Court House Square, Bardstown

LOUISIANA: Antoine's, 713 St. Louis St., New Orleans

MAINE: Jordan Pond House, Seal Harbor; **Sunset Farm,** Basin Point, South Harpswell; **Worster House,** Hallowell

MARYLAND: Kitty Knight House, U.S. 213, Georgetown; **Normandy Farm,** State Highway 189, Rockville

MASSACHUSETTS: Andover Inn, Chapel Ave., Andover; **Brookfield Inn,** Brookfield; **Colonial Inn,** 11 Monument Sq., Concord; **1812 House,** 11 Salem End Road, Framingham Center; **Four High Road,** 4 High Road, Newbury; **General Glover Inn,** U.S. 1A, Swampscott; **Hartwell Farm,** Virginia Road, Concord; **Old Chase House,** State Highway 28, West Harwich, Cape Cod; **Old Mill,** State Highway 2, Westminster; **Parker House,** 60 School St. at Tremont, Boston; **Publick House,** Main St., Sturbridge; **Towne Lyne House,** Newburyport Turnpike, Lynnfield; **Union Oyster House,** 41 Union St., Boston; **Wayside Inn,** U.S. 20, South Sudbury; **White Drum,** Intersection of State Highways 2 and 78, Orange; **Wiggins Old Tavern,** 36 King St., Northampton; **Williams Inn,** College Place, Williamstown; **Wright Tavern,** 2 Lexington Road, Concord

MICHIGAN: Bit of Sweden, Norton Hotel, 410 Griswold, Detroit; **Botsford Inn,** 28000 Grand River, Farmington; **Dearborn Inn,** 20301 Oakwood Blvd., Dearborn; **Devon Gables,** U.S. 24, Bloomfield Hills; **Fox and Hounds Inn,** U.S. 10, Bloomfield Hills; **Holiday House,** U.S. 12, St. Joseph; **Phil De Graff's Lodges,** Trout Lake; **Pontchartrain Wine Cellars,** 618 Wayne St., Detroit; **Red Brick Tavern,** U.S. 131, Plainwell; **St. Clair Inn,** 500 North Riverside Ave., St. Clair; **Sid's Restaurant,** 9715 St. Clair River Drive, Algonac

MINNESOTA: **Covered Wagon,** 114 South Fourth St., Minneapolis; **Lowell Inn,** Stillwater; **Lutsen Resort,** Lutsen

MISSISSIPPI: **Angelo's,** 3206 West Beach, Gulfport; **Old Southern Tea Room,** 1201 Monroe St., Vicksburg

MISSOURI: **Arrow Rock Tavern,** Arrow Rock; **Club Continental,** 415 North 12th Blvd., St. Louis; **Edmonds,** 3185 Gravois Ave., St. Louis; **Grecian Gardens,** 205 South Sixth St., St. Louis; **Happy Hollow Ranch,** Long Beach Road, Branson; **Hotel Taneycomo,** Rockaway Beach

NEBRASKA: **Hotel Cornhusker,** Thirteenth and N Sts., Lincoln

NEW HAMPSHIRE: **Peckett's-on-Sugar Hill,** Franconia; **Pine Wood Inn and Cottages,** State Highway 11, New Durham; **Walpole Inn,** State Highway 12, Walpole; **Wentworth-by-the-Sea,** Portsmouth

NEW JERSEY: **Colligan's Stockton Inn,** Bridge and Main Sts., Stockton; **Old Mill Inn,** U.S. 202, Bernardsville; **William Pitt,** 94 Main St., Chatham

NEW MEXICO: **Hacienda Dining Room,** Old Town Plaza, Old Albuquerque

NEW YORK: **Bird and Bottle Inn,** U.S. 9, Garrison; **Blue Spruce Inn,** 1480 Northern Blvd., Roslyn, L. I.; **Dahlstrom's Green Tree Lodge,** 93 West Jericho Turnpike, Huntington Station, L. I.; **Emily Shaw's,** State Highway 137, Poundridge; **Gage and Tollner's,** 372-4 Fulton St., Brooklyn; **Georgian Inn,** Jericho Turnpike, Huntington, L. I.; **Hampshire House,** 150 Central Park South, New York; **Hastings House,** State Highway 11, Homer; **Krebs,** 39 West Genessee St., Skaneateles; **Leighton's Woodlands Lake Restaurant,** Saw Mill River Parkway, Ardsley; **Maine Maid,** State Highways 106-107, Jericho, L. I.; **Memory Inn,** State Highway 9, Poughkeepsie; **Mirror Lake Inn,** 35 Lakeshore Drive, Lake Placid; **Nelson House,** 28-42 Market St., Poughkeepsie; **Old Drover's Inn,** State Highway 22, Dover Plains; **Sportsman's Tavern,** State Highway 28, Cooperstown; **Spring House,** 3001 Monroe Ave., Rochester; **Tavern on the Green,** 67th St. and Central Park West, New York; **Town and Country,** 284 Park Avenue, New York; **Waldorf-Astoria,** Park Ave. and 50th St., New York; **Wendover Farms,** State Highway 9, Wappingers Falls; **Ye Olde Chop House,** 118 Cedar St., New York.

NORTH CAROLINA: **Holly Inn,** Pinehurst; **Nu-Wray Inn,** U.S. 19E, Burnsville; **Sunset Farm,** U.S. 19, Whittier; **Tapoco Lodge,** U.S. 129, Tapoco

NOVA SCOTIA: **Green Shutters,** Rural Route 1, Mahone Bay

OHIO: **Gourmet Restaurant,** Sixth St. between Vine and Race, Cincinnati; **Hotel Phoenix Coffee Shoppe,** 305 South Main St., Findlay; **Red Brick Tavern,** U.S. 40, London; **Restaurant Continentale,** Fifth and Race Sts., Cincinnati; **Spanish Inn,** 15 East Eighth St., Cincinnati; **Tivoli,** 4535 Monroe St., Toledo; **Valerio's Italian Restaurant,** 114 East Sixth St. (second floor), Cincinnati

OREGON: Oregon Caves Château, Oregon Caves; Oregon Oyster Co., 208 Southwest Ankeny St., Portland

PENNSYLVANIA: Bookbinder's Restaurant, 125 Walnut St., Philadelphia; Pocono Manor, Pocono Manor; River House, River Road, New Hope; Shartlesville Hotel, State Highway 22, Shartlesville; Stevens House, South Prince and West King Sts., Lancaster; Tarello's Restaurant, 1623 Chestnut St., Philadelphia; Tow Path House, New Hope; Water Wheel Inn, Old U.S. 611, Doylestown

QUEBEC: Au Petit Robinson, Isle Bizzard; Château Frontenac, Quebec City

SOUTH CAROLINA: Brewton Inn and Tea Room, 75 Church St., Charleston; Gold Eagle, Box 468, Beaufort; Poinsett Hotel, South Main St., Greenville

TENNESSEE: Buckhorn Inn, R.F.D. #1, Gatlinburg; Cupboard Tea Room, 124 North Spring St., Murfreesboro; New Gatlinburg Inn, State Highway 71, Gatlinburg; Norris Park Tea Room, Norris Dam, Norris

TEXAS: Bill Wood's Famous Foods, At the Circle, Waco; Casa de Palmas Hotel, 113 North Main St., McAllen; Del Camino Coffee Shop, 500 El Paso Drive, El Paso; Granger's, Sabine Pass; Kelley's, 910 Texas, Houston; Original Mexican Restaurant, 117 Losoya St., San Antonio; Shamrock Hotel, Main at Holcombe, Houston; Tarpon Inn, Port Aransas, Mustang Island

UTAH: Beau Brummel, Salt Lake City; El Rancho Cordova, 543 West Third North, Salt Lake City; Newhouse Hotel, Fourth and Main Sts.,

Salt Lake City; Parry Lodge, U.S. 89, Kanab

VERMONT: Barrows House, State Highway 30, Dorset; Windham County Hotel, State Highway 30, Newfane

VIRGINIA: Halfway House, U.S. 1, Richmond; Hotel Raleigh, Ninth and Bank Sts., Richmond; Skyline Terrace Restaurant, Skyline Drive, Front Royal; Town House, South High St., Franklin; Virginian Hotel, Intersection U.S. 29 and 460, Lynchburg; Williamsburg Lodge, South England St., Williamsburg

WASHINGTON: Camlin Hotel, Ninth and Pine, Seattle; Crabapple, Bellevue Shopping Square, Seattle; Dupuis Tavern, U.S. 101, Port Angeles; Green Hut, State Highway 2, Coulee Dam; King Oscar's Smörgasbord, 4312 Aurora Ave., Seattle; Lake Crescent Lodge, U.S. 101, Port Angeles; Maison Blanc, 306-308 Marion St., Seattle; Ruby Chow's Chinese Dinner Club, Broadway and Jefferson Sts., Seattle; Shamrock Inn, U.S. 99, Chehalis

WEST VIRGINIA: General Lewis Hotel, Intersection U.S. 60 and 219, Lewisburg; Park View Inn, Berkeley Springs

WISCONSIN: Brad Ryan's Lake Breeze Lodge, County Trunk X, Three Lakes; Fallhall Glen, R.R. 5, Black River Falls; Fish Shanty, Port Washington; Fox and Hounds, Hubertus; Mader's Famous Restaurant, 1041 North Third St., Milwaukee

WYOMING: Noble Hotel, Third and Main Sts., Lander